Everything (almost)
In Its Place

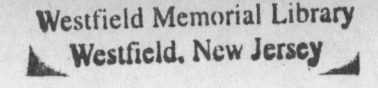
Alicia Rockmore and Sarah Welch

Everything (almost) In Its Place

Control Chaos, Conquer Clutter, and Get Organized the Buttoned Up Way

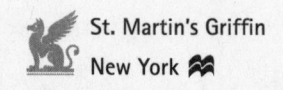
St. Martin's Griffin
New York

www.stmartins.com

Book design by Ralph Fowler / rlf design

Library of Congress Cataloging-in-Publication Data

Rockmore, Alicia.
   Everything (almost) in its place : control chaos, conquer clutter, and get organized the buttoned up way / Alicia Rockmore and Sarah Welch. —1st ed.
      p. cm.
  ISBN-13: 978-0-312-37350-4
  ISBN-10: 0-312-37350-3
  1. House cleaning. 2. Orderliness. 3. Storage in the home. I. Welch, Sarah. II. Title.
  TX324.R6145 2008
  648—dc22   2008013010

First Edition: August 2008

10 9 8 7 6 5 4 3 2 1

Contents

Contents

vi

Acknowledgments

A huge thank-you first of all to my cohort and close friend, Sarah Welch. I cannot believe how lucky I am to have you to partner and work with. You are a truly talented individual.

Deb Merion, Jane Dystel, and Miriam Goderich, thank you for the support, organization, and help in getting this book together. I know we could not have done this without you.

To the other two cofounders of Buttoned Up, Inc., Susan Lerner and Nancy Meyer. You are my sisters, my second and third mothers, and business partners. You mean the world to me.

Thank you to the entire Buttoned Up, Inc., team: Hollie, Ashleigh, Carolyn, Cory, Gina, Cindy, Greg, Anne Marie, Jessica, Lauren, Charly, Corrie, Alan, and so on . . . I am blessed to work with these talented individuals and without them Buttoned Up would still be just a dream.

To my husband, Adam, and adorable daughter, Lucy. You make me smile each and every day. Your support of me and my work means the world to me and I hope I can make you proud. I love you.

Marissa Logan, Brigg, Emma, Harry, Chace, James, Caroline, Megan, Corbin, Alex, Dustin, Shayna, Rachel, Baby Hill, and I am sure one or two others before this book is published: You are my nieces and nephews and some of the greatest gifts in my life. I love you all very much, Auntie E.

Cyndi Manzo, Marci Miller, Angela Harris, Liz Paley, Amy Lerner-Hill, and Kimberly Lerner: I could not ask for closer friends or a better support system. Thank you for the advice, shoulders to lean on, and love.

A special thank-you to my mom and dad. I know my dad is looking down on me right now and smiling.

Finally, to all of the countless friends, acquaintances, contacts, investors, businesswomen, and entrepreneurs who took the time to help us nurture Buttoned Up and bring it to life. We could not be where we are today without you. From the bottom of my heart. Thank you!

—*Alicia Rockmore*

Holy cow, Alicia, we did it!! Thank you for being the Yin to my Yang (or is it Yang to my Yin?), for keeping us so steadily on track, and for being the world's best cheerleader, Energizer Bunny, and partner in crime. I'm so lucky to be able to work with you and to count you as one of my closest friends.

To Gardiner and Will, thank you for allowing me to disappear at night and during nap windows on weekends to write without complaining. Thank you for cheering me on when I was tired. Thank you for believing that we had something interesting to say. It takes enormous reserves of patience and a degree of selflessness to give someone the space and encouragement to pursue the muse and I will always be grateful to both of you for that. The two of you are the lights of my life.

To Nancy Meyer and Susan Lerner, without you Buttoned Up, and this book, would not exist. To Mom and Dad, thank you for your unending support, wisdom, and unconditional love. To Deb Merion, your coaching was essential. To the Buttoned Up team: Hollie, Cindy, Anne Marie, Gina, Jess, Lauren,

Ashleigh, Cory, Carolyn, Charly, Corrie, Alan, et al.—your ideas, your talents, and your incredible energy have made dreams come true. Thank you.

And finally to all the people whose support along the way made it possible to do this: Pansey Burke, Lauren Arvonio, Jane Dystel, Miriam Goderich, Elizabeth Payne, Ted McCagg, Kieran Juska, Sonal Shah, Adam Rockmore, Todd Smith, Ann Smith, Liz Gruzkievicz, Amy Keroes, Amy Stanton, Irina Barinov, Kevin Travis, Joshua Kanter, Travis Bowen, Valeska von Schirmeister, and Teresita Reyes.

—Sarah Welch

Acknowledgments

Everything (almost)
In Its Place

Introduction: Our Story

t was 8:00 A.M. on a clear February morning in 2004 when the seed of an idea that would transform our lives took root. We were meeting in the big corporate cafeteria of the building where Alicia worked, lamenting the fact that it had taken us a ridiculous amount of time—three long months of schedule juggling and rain checks—to finally schedule breakfast together. We were both drowning in endless lists of *should-do's* and *must-do's* that left little room for the things that really matter, like catching up with an old friend.

As we joked about putting "get a life" on our to-do lists and counseled each other on our respective situations, we couldn't help but notice the similarities in our problems. Despite our different organizational styles (Alicia is detail oriented and list driven, while Sarah is more of a focus-on-the-big-picture and let's-just-keep-moving-in-the-right-direction type of gal) both of us felt out of control, disorganized, and overwhelmed. Sarah wondered how Alicia could feel stressed when it appeared that she had every single thing she would ever need to do on one of her many lists. Alicia marveled at the fact that Sarah was actually anxious when she seemed to instinctively handle most of her life's to-do's in her head.

As we compared notes, we realized we had both purchased many of the same organizing products, read the same magazine articles, and listened to the same experts about how to "do it all." Yet here we were, both miserable! We realized that whatever we were doing to get organized was not working and was actually making us *more* anxious!

Alicia hated that the filing, calendar, and closet-organizing systems she'd tried were too compartmentalized and too specialized to be integrated into one workable system and took so much time to learn that they became another full-time job. In order to get one organizational task completed, she needed to cobble together three or four separate systems. In the end it was often easier to raise the white flag and surrender. She wanted to feel as though her life's many details, like genes on a string of DNA, all added up to something unified and meaningful. She yearned for a manageable road map to guide her in keeping her busy life together.

Sarah, meanwhile, was tired of having her hopes dashed each time a "perfect" organizational solution failed to live up to its promise (or rather, each time she failed to make it work). She fantasized about living the life of one of those superwomen who managed to both excel at work and be a model mom, wife, friend, sister, and daughter. She tried any product and followed any expert advertising "the answer." In the meantime, she kept falling off the organizational wagon and into chaos when a perfectly reasonable bump in the road of her packed life, like a sick child, would throw her "just-in-time" schedule off. Sarah, a management consultant by day—and budding entrepreneur at night, during nap windows on weekends, and every free moment in between—had a hectic travel schedule and an agenda that was dictated by her clients. Her organizational weakness was tracking details, like did she pay the utilities bill or remember a friend's birthday with a card and a phone call? After years of frustrating dead ends, she simply longed for a practical solution that she could actually work into her packed life to manage the details more effectively without losing sight of the big picture.

So there we were: two intelligent, professional women, trapped in what we now like to call "organizer hell." There had to be a better way.

A few months and a zillion iced teas and lattes later, we founded Buttoned Up, Inc. (enlisting the help of Alicia's two sisters, Nancy and Susan). Our mission is to help stretched and stressed women like us get the fundamentals organized so they have more time and energy to enjoy life. We make organizational products and create content designed to help women stop chasing the illusion of organizational perfection and get happily, practically Buttoned Up. Along the way, we've spoken to hundreds of women from all over the country, of all ages and lifestyles about their organizational challenges, and the majority agree: chasing organizational perfection is exhausting and disheartening. Until now organizational perfection has been held up as the sole option for women who want to banish household clutter, have a neat but functional playroom, and keep an easy and practical family calendar. It's an all-or-nothing world.

This book offers a revolutionary approach to getting and staying organized. The idea: you get more done by organizing less. That's right, when it comes to organizing, we will show you how less is more. We've even given our philosophy a revolutionary name: Imperfect Organization.

Quiz: What's Your Organizational Style?

1. My to-do list holds...

    a. Everything from "brush my teeth" to "lock the doors."

    b. The things I must get done to stay on track.

    c. What list?

2. I treat my to-do's...

    a. With equality; everything gets done regardless of its importance or urgency.

    b. With equity; I attend to my to-do's based on importance, urgency, people counting on me, etc.

    c. With immediate attention; I address each to-do as it presents itself.

3. I'm most frustrated when...

    a. I don't get to cross off my entire list before I go to bed.

    b. I waste time power-washing the deck when I really need to finish a presentation for my boss.

    c. I realize there is something to get done right before I am heading to bed.

4. To feel organized, I must...

    a. Cross off "feed the dog," "go to the bank," and "run the garbage disposal" every day.

    b. Stay focused on making progress toward my goals.

    c. Put out each fire that comes my way.

Quiz: What's Your Organizational Style?

5. My current organizational system is...

    a. Too structured and unforgiving; I'm never available for a spontaneous cup of coffee with a friend.

    b. On track but it takes effort to stay that way.

    c. Just-in-time.

If you answered mostly A: You're the do-it-all person, so much so that you become a slave to your list. You tend to move top to bottom without any rhyme or reason to the list order. Your ability to get things done and keep track of your to-do's is a strength. But your overly structured plans and inability to take things off your list can make fitting to-do's around your everyday life a challenge. Keep reading for tips on how to prioritize your list, saving you time for the things you really want to do!

If you answered mostly B: You are the prioritizer. You make sure to take care of the urgent and important things on your list each day, but forget the rest and opt to spend that time with friends, family, or yourself. This book will show you that delegation is the key to getting these priorities (and some less crucial items) accomplished!

If you answered mostly C: You are the firefighter. You tend to deal with your to-do's as they present themselves, putting out one fire at a time. You often feel behind the ball and wish you could get organized enough to decrease the urgency of everything that comes across your plate. Read on for help determining which to-do's are crucial and which can be ignored or postponed.

In this book, we deliver organizational tips and tricks that are effective because they fit into busy, "sandwiched" lives. We are all women of the "sandwiched generation." We are busy and stressed-out so we often feel sandwiched between personal and professional lives and the needs of children, spouses, and even older parents. We intuitively know that becoming organized will give us more of what we want: lowered stress levels and more peace of mind. These are tips that have worked for us and hundreds of other women. We won't overload you with complicated formulas for calculating priorities or preset formats that force you to organize according to our rules or impossible standards. Instead, we will present our proven ideas about getting "unstuck" and moving forward toward getting organized.

Our secrets for getting organized are different, because we don't obsess about what you need to do—we simply tell you what you *don't* need to do.

We're a bit contrary and aren't like other get-organized plans because we feel that letting go will help you get Buttoned Up, and being Buttoned Up means you have confidently and easily organized the most important tasks on your list, giving yourself permission to forget the rest.

Three Secrets to Getting Buttoned Up

Secret #1: You don't need to be perfect.

Secret #2: You don't need to do everything on your lists.

Secret #3: You don't need to do everything yourself.

On the surface, it may sound simple, but simple ideas are sometimes the hardest to enact. Because learning new ways of thinking and behaving takes practice, we'll walk you through each step with real-life examples and plenty of practice for each new skill.

Add our three secrets together and integrate the Buttoned Up skills into your life, and we know you'll be more organized. You will feel more firmly in the driver's seat, clearer about where you're going in your life, and more prepared for the journey. Or, as we say, you'll become more Buttoned Up.

We are both challenged to stay organized every day. Alicia struggles to let go of low-priority items on her to-do list, while Sarah struggles to stay organized in a healthy, balanced way. We know it's not easy. But we love the challenge of becoming better organized, because it gives us more time to taste the sweetness in life . . . a movie date with our husbands, snuggling our kids, or chatting with girlfriends over coffee. We like to call the free time we get as a result of being Buttoned Up "BU Time." Say it out loud and it's "be you time." In other words, BU Time is the time to be yourself and do the things you enjoy, secure in the knowledge that the many tasks in your life are well taken care of.

Who We Are

We are two busy, working moms with hectic, full lives. We both worried we were not organized enough but struggled to find the time and energy to get started on an organizing program. We understand the piles, the junk, the expensive organizational gadgets that go unused, and have partners who seem as flummoxed about staying on top of the chaos as we are. The approaches we have developed celebrate the notion of Imperfect Organization—as a way of doing more by organizing less. These tips and techniques have been road-tested by our friends, family members, and hundreds of busy women across the United States. They have worked for so many that we decided to help more women by writing this book.

This book also benefits from our divergent organizational styles and perspectives. Alicia is one of the lucky few who are preternaturally organized—she was born with the organizational gene! She knows how to get things done and makes whatever needs doing a priority, sometimes to a fault. Sarah, on the other hand, struggles a bit more with maintaining organization, joking that she's an "organizational wannabe." Our two different styles and perspectives play off of each other and deliver an approach that is entirely human, multidimensional, and, we hope, fun. Some readers may be more like Sarah, some more like Alicia, and many somewhere in between. No matter where you fall on the organizational spectrum, you will find information here that will help you tame your to-do list and start living!

Everything (almost) In Its Place tells how to live an organized life, not a life overrun by organization.

Remember the Three Buttoned Up Secrets:

Secret #1: You don't need to be perfect.

Secret #2: You don't need to do everything on your lists.

Secret #3: You don't need to do everything yourself.

Ditch Perfection

Over the past few years we have spoken to quite a few women across America about organization, disorganization, and every state in between. They have invited us into their homes, spoken to us at length on the phone, and patiently filled out surveys. Thank heavens organization is a topic that seems to be as much fun to talk about as it is to research. Women are absolutely effusive about the subject!

One refrain we heard more than anything else was, "I worry I'm not organized *enough*." In fact, a staggering 80 percent of women agree with this statement. Just think about that for a second: your neighbor or friend who you believe is supremely organized is just as likely to believe she's not organized as your friend who is, well, struggling a little bit with the concept. How is that possible? We weren't sure.

It got us thinking and asking more questions. What exactly does it mean to you to be Buttoned Up? Does it mean having all the things in your house, like the items in your makeup drawer, meticulously categorized and contained? Does it mean having a floor you can eat off of? A workspace that's utterly free of clutter? A to-do list with every single item crossed off by the end of the day? Anticipating every number your boss will need before she asks for them? Being able to throw an impromptu, but warm, gathering of family and friends at 7:00 P.M. on a Tuesday without breaking a sweat? Paying the bills on time? Your family photos organized into albums by year? Never failing to send a friend a birthday card? Making sure your child always has a cheering section at their soccer games? Having the time to exercise every day?

Your response may be all of those things or none of them. It all depends because organization and the benefits it brings is a very subjective and personal concept. It means different things to different people and it looks different at age thirty-five than it does at twenty-five or sixty-five. It looks different for singles and couples, moms of toddlers and empty nesters. But even though there are thousands of different definitions, for the most part all of us feel like we're at least a little shy of where we really need to be or should be in our lives. Somehow we all feel we could be *more* Buttoned Up. Why is that?

As we culled our notes, synthesized and summarized findings, and discussed our own struggles with the concept, we realized that we all have, somewhere in the dark recesses of our minds, an "organizational yardstick" against which we measure ourselves. This organizational standard is probably not something you actively, consciously put there. Most of us don't even realize we have one. But it *is* there, and until you realize it, you are at its mercy.

Our friend Amy Keroes, mother, lawyer, wife, founder of the company MommyTrackd.com, and all-around amazing person, summarized the dilemma simply and elegantly. She said, "I think we all have tape recordings in our head telling us what it means to be organized without even realizing it. Mine loops the message: 'a messy room is a messy mind.' My father used to tell us that all the time when we were kids. He was probably just trying to get us to do our fair share of the housework, but I subconsciously picked it up, and like it or not, here I am thirty years later living that mantra. I don't function unless things are neat and tidy. So, whether or not I have the time, I feel compelled to spend some part of my day tidying up. Sometimes I wish I could just let it go."

That internal yardstick has the potential to make you a little crazy. It also has the potential to make you suffer.

Let's start with the crazy. Sometimes, our internal yardstick, much like Amy's, makes us feel compelled to do things—and do them in a certain way. It's like we're powerless to change the routine and often unable to get moving on anything else until that thing is done just the right way. Liz, another incredible (and incredibly busy) mom we spoke to, joked about her compulsive bed-making habit. "Every morning, I absolutely, positively *must* make the beds before I can leave the house. And they have to be made just so. No wrinkles, no lumps, corners tucked in, top sheet folded over . . . you get the picture. My six-year-old twins try to help me by making their beds before school, but I often find myself sneaking in to 'fix' the beds after the kids catch the bus. I don't know why, but the beds have to be made, and made the right way, before I can relax and face the day."

Sarah's a little crazy too, by her own admission, when it comes to doing the laundry. Her "thing" is folding the clean clothes. "For some reason, I feel compelled to fold everything just so. Shirts must be faceup, free of all wrinkles, and 'balanced,' with the sleeves equidistant from in the center. Towels need to be folded in half, then half again, and only then can each side be folded in toward the center. If someone else has thoughtfully folded the clothes for me as Liz remakes the beds, I often refold at least the shirts before I can put things away. I don't know why I feel compelled to do this, but I do."

Ann, a New Hampshire mom juggling two children under the age of three, is militant about the way the dishwasher must be loaded. "It's a mystery to me how I got to be so strict about loading the dishwasher. But I'm totally guilty of unloading, re-rinsing, and reloading it if my husband or a house guest does it the wrong way. I guess food particles on plates and cutlery that are supposed to be clean really gross me out."

"I don't know why, but . . ." is a big clue that you've got a little crazy problem. Whether it's remaking beds, refolding clothes, or redistributing the dishes in the dishwasher, if you feel compelled to do something even if you know there are other, more productive things you could be or should be doing—you're at the mercy of an organizational yardstick.

Sometimes an organizational yardstick creates more of an intimidation than a compulsion. Often we set such an impossible standard for ourselves that we never even attempt to reach it. For example, you know you should be doing something, like getting your important information organized in case of an emergency, but you just can't ever seem to get yourself over the hump to do anything about it. Every time you walk past your filing cabinet, you shudder, your brow furrows, or your shoulders tense up—but you keep walking, unable to overcome your organizational inertia.

Deb from Michigan, a wife, mother of two, and professional writer, told us how she suffered over her messy desk. "I'm the kind of person who likes to spread my papers out so I can see everything. It looks messy, but I can only work when everything is at my fingertips. I try to neaten up when I'm done by making piles, but I never have the neat desk or office I'd like. I have a huge backlog of random papers that I don't want to spend time filing and don't want to toss. I've got a block."

Alicia's sister Nancy, has a block about filing photos. "I'm so embarrassed. I love taking pictures of my kids, so I have stacks of them. I really want to put them into scrapbooks with things like pieces of their artwork, and I get inspired when I look at my friends who have beautifully organized and displayed albums. But for some reason, I just don't ever seem to find the time."

"I know I should, but . . ." is another clue that you're suffering. It indicates that there is a gap between what you believe you are supposed to be and who you actually are.

What is it about these organizational yardsticks that causes craziness and suffering? Well, it's not the yardsticks themselves. You can't accomplish much without some definition of what you want to achieve. So, yardsticks are necessary; but if you are beating yourself up trying to live by your particular yardstick, that is a problem. The key is to find a yardstick that matches your lifestyle and goals.

How Seeking Someone Else's Version of Perfection Keeps Us from Getting Buttoned Up

The real question is *who defines these yardsticks*? If you aren't actively choosing what it means to you to be Buttoned Up, then who is? Well, as with all things (for example, weight loss), there is no shortage of experts who are more than happy to step into the breach and answer the question for you.

For starters, there are always our parents. Often we pick

Imperfect Organization

Letting go of someone else's idea of perfect organization makes perfect sense if it allows you to get done what needs getting done. Anne Lamott, author of *Bird by Bird*, says "I used to not be able to work if there were dishes in the sink. Then I had a child and now I can work if there is a corpse in the sink." You can be organized without being *perfectly* organized. Imperfect organization is a novel concept that examines organization within the broader context of your total life. The basic idea is that in order to get more sanely Buttoned Up overall, you may need to let go of the need to be perfectly organized in some areas of your life.

Organizational approaches and "solutions" promoted today focus on just one aspect of your life, like your work agenda or your closet, and aim to get that one area absolutely, perfectly in order. Unfortunately, life isn't easily compartmentalized. What most people need help with is getting *the big picture* Buttoned Up. If you try to apply rigid, compartmentalized systems to your entire life, getting organized becomes a full-time job. Since time is one thing most of us just don't have to spare, there has to be a better option.

We've noticed that when you let go of working toward being perfectly organized, great things happen. You can still maintain high standards, but letting go of the control needed to reach perfection lets you focus on organization as a satisfying tool to obtain and maintain what's important to you. It also enables others in your life to help you. Last but definitely not least, when you spend less time getting perfectly organized, you have more BU Time—more time to be you.

up on and repeat the organizational standards that our parents have set. We live with them for nearly twenty years, and have it drummed into our heads that "this is the way we like it, so that's the way it's going to be done, *thank you very much*." It's no wonder that we adopt their organizational tics and habits as if it's our genetic destiny. The problem is, you're not your parents! You're you: a marvelous combination of both, but greater than the sum of the individual parts. Don't assume their definition of organization is right for you. On this same note, when you create a new household it is likely that you and your partner will have different opinions of what it means to be Buttoned Up. We suggest you work to reconcile them rather than working to live up to one another's unrealistic expectations.

Then, there's a little something we like to call "Org Porn." Org Porn, in a nutshell, is that glossy, airbrushed, fantasy world where everything is pristine, serene, and perfectly in order. It's everywhere you look: magazines, coffee table books, advertisements, and TV shows. We have to admit, it's soothing to meditate over those beautiful photos of meticulously organized things and consider taking on a few of the "bite-sized" projects that are typically illustrated. We love those TV shows where professionals convert clutter disasters into paragons of order. While it may be titillating and spur us to take some action, be clear: ultimately it is pure fantasy. Measuring yourself by that fantasy yardstick will not only ensure that getting organized becomes yet another full-time job, it's guaranteed to make you feel like a failure. Why? Because that airbrushed land of perfect organization cannot be sustained in this messy, unpredictable world called real life.

Finally, there are those people (friends, family, and experts) who are just so darn good at staying on top of it all. Most of us have at least someone in our lives who has more than one of these qualities:

- Never forgets to send a birthday card on time (and who picks out the really funny ones, too)

- Always has a tin of home-baked cookies on hand

- Has a home that looks picture-perfect

- Seems to reply to your e-mail before you even send it

- Exercises more than you do

- Decorates beautifully for every holiday

- Cooks fresh, delicious meals

- Maintains lush green houseplants or a glowing garden

- Can find anything she needs in her house in five minutes or less

- Has never missed an opportunity to be with or watch her children perform (whether she works out of the home or not)

- Is the queen of community involvement as a room mother, PTA president, board member, or synagogue/church volunteer

- Sends out her holiday cards by December 10—and everyone in the family photo is wearing matching outfits

- Contacts you more than you contact her

- Always looks chic and stylish

- Makes more money than you do

We admire these paragons of organization and togetherness, and we're a bit jealous too, because they seem to be doing something we're not. Clearly, they are winning the secret competition that every woman knows exists, even though no one ever talks about it: there is an evaluation committee, somewhere, we're pretty sure, who is rating every woman on her productivity. At the end of every day, the committee holds up scorecards from 1–9, like in an ice-skating competition. We worry that we're the one who is left sitting on the ice—is it possible to score a perfect 0?

Look carefully at who is defining your yardstick. Do you have a little case of the crazies? Are you suffering from the *should-do* syndrome? Those are the telltale signs that you're trying to measure up to someone else's standard. The first step in getting Buttoned Up is to take charge and create a yardstick for yourself.

Your Goal

The goal is for you to *feel* in control and to *be* in control. The two are inextricably linked: Buttoned Up is both a state of mind and a state of being.

In that respect, getting Buttoned Up is a lot like getting to a healthy weight. The trick to getting and staying that way is to let go of others' yardsticks (it's 124 pounds, it's a BMI of 19, it's having six-pack abs, it's fitting into a size 6, it's a closet categorized by color and style, it's a pristine desk, it's never being late, it's making the beds the right way) and define your own. Says Pam, "As soon as I stopped defining my 'ideal weight' as a single number, a static goal, and instead defined it first as a *positive state of mind* (being happily fit) and then as an *acceptable range* of numbers (no, I'm not telling), staying trim became much easier. Sometimes my figure is leaner and more outwardly perfect, and sometimes it's a little rounder and softer. But I never feel like I'm failing. And that's what keeps me on track. The same holds true for getting organized."

How you feel about what you do affects what you do. The only way to feel and be in control is to actively define what being Buttoned Up means to you. Let go of those definitions set by others. Let go of the illusion of perfection and the tyranny of rigid rules. Stop reacting. All that does is make you crazy, make you suffer, or a little of both.

You might just be scratching your head and thinking, "I'm sorry, how is this going to help me find my passport lost in a stack of papers somewhere in my house?" The answer is simple: letting go of others' yardsticks and replacing them with your own will get you unstuck. It will enable you to change the way you file important documents, keep your calendar, keep your lists, prioritize your time, and keep track of your stuff. Better yet, it'll help you stay Buttoned Up over time in an Imperfectly Organized way.

Using someone else's organizational yardstick, like an umbrella over our heads on a sunny day, darkens our feelings about how organized we are, no matter how well we're actually doing.

Stop Chasing Someone Else's Idea of Perfection

We want to help you set your own yardstick. One that makes sense for you and will help you stay Buttoned Up over the long haul. The ultimate goal is to help you have more time and energy to do the things you want, not to do more organizing.

It's time to let go of some of those tasks that don't really matter in the long run. These are the tasks that won't really improve the quality of your life or make getting tasks completed any easier. They mostly instill a tyranny of perfection that keeps you stuck trying to achieve it or stuck because you can't. Of course, you're the only one who knows what it is that you can truly let go. Some common perfection "ideas" (usually inspired by Org Porn) to get you thinking:

1. Arranging clothes closets so that like items (e.g., skirts, pants) are all hung on exactly the same type of hanger

2. Organizing your linen closet so that it is color coordinated and grouped according to size and shape (e.g., twin green fitted sheets, queen white flat sheets)

3. Alphabetizing your CDs and DVDs

4. Making sure that two cars can actually fit in your two-car garage

5. Taking food staples like flour, cereal, and sugar out of their original packaging and putting them in matching canisters

6. Making a complete fancy scrapbook for every child and for every holiday

7. Cataloging and dating every piece of your children's art

8. Cataloging via Dewey decimal system all of the books in your house

9. Being able to fold T-shirts like you are a Gap employee

10. Having a completely clear desk

Again, you may not suffer from trying to achieve any of the particulars of the above, but we're willing to bet you have some unrealistic goals that may be getting in your way.

Why Get Buttoned Up?

One way to clarify your objectives is to simply ask yourself: why did I buy this book?

Please take a minute to write your reason here. Don't think about it too long. Just think about what was exactly in your brain when you picked this book up off the virtual or actual shelf of your bookstore.

_____

_____

Rest assured, whatever your reason is, it's a great one! Following are a few more questions. As with the first one, don't think too long about your answer. Simply read the question, and write the first thoughts that come to mind. Those thoughts will be the most honest and helpful moving forward.

Another great way to focus on the "why" is to project yourself forward in time. Imagine that you are ninety years old, reflecting on your life and generally proud of the person that you have chosen to be. What are the top ten most important things you have done/become?

1. _____

2. _____

3. _____

4. _____

5. _____

6. _____

7. _____

8. _____

9. _____

10. _____

Now, take a moment to reflect on those goals. What aspects of your life do you need to get organized in order to accomplish/become your dreams?

_____

_____

_____

_____

_____

We advise you to copy the above list and hang it up in a place you see every day. That will project your goals prominently into your mind and motivate you as you read through the book.

Finally, list here the three or four things you have been holding on to that you can let go. Make this your initial list of to-do's you will ditch. For example: "Scrapbook baby book for my now five-year-old daughter" and "Alphabetize DVDs and CDs."

_____

_____

_____

_____

These exercises are the first step to ditching perfection and letting go of your organizational yardstick. Use your responses to these exercises as a springboard for getting Buttoned Up. Start the to-do's that will move you closer to your goal of organization, and forget about the things that eat away your time with little payoff.

Button 1: Ditch Perfection

Being Buttoned Up is not about being perfect or doing everything yourself. It's about the joy and peace of mind that comes with being prepared and knowing how and when to let go, so that you can handle the inevitable twists and turns on the road of life with confidence and sanity intact.

Don't follow someone else's organizational yardstick (which we can adopt from our parents, Org Porn, or family or friends).

The real payoff in getting organized is not perfection but BU Time—time to be you.

Letting go of others' yardsticks and replacing them with your own will get you unstuck.

Set your own yardstick by:

1. Letting go of tasks that don't matter in the long run.

2. Clarifying your own objectives (why did you buy this book?).

3. Determining what you need to organize in order to accomplish your dreams, and looking at your list every day.

You Don't Have to Do Everything on Your List

(Just the 20 Percent that Really Matters)

Have you ever laid awake in bed wondering how you were going to get everything done that you needed to do? If you have, you're not alone. According to the National Center for Health Statistics, 60 percent of Americans feel they do not have enough time to get everything done.[1] Fortunately, as Alicia laid awake in bed one morning, a simple, elegant solution for handling this dilemma came to her. That compelling idea—that you don't have to do everything on your lists—became the second of Buttoned Up's three secrets.

One oppressively hot and sticky New York morning, the digital desk clock's big, red numbers shouted 6:18 A.M. as Alicia reached for one of her six legal-sized notepads. Like the other five pads, it was overflowing with lists of things she needed to do. Her eyes glazed over as she stared at the pad with her work to-do's. As a newly promoted marketing director, she had three internal meetings to prepare for, one call to make to smooth the ruffled feathers of an important agency partner, a trip to visit West Coast customers, and a schedule so full of meetings it left her no time to think. She was overwhelmed.

With a sigh, she pushed back from the desk and meandered to the kitchen to pour herself a tall, cold glass of iced tea. "Usually when I'm stuck, iced tea gives me the boost I need to plow through," said Alicia. "But it didn't work this time. When I came back to the lists, I found that I was just paralyzed, which is not normal for me at all. My eyes would read over the words on the page, but as I flipped through the sheets, I found I couldn't focus on any one thing and almost as soon as I read something, I forgot it.

"It was immensely frustrating. On the one hand, I couldn't sleep because I was so anxious about everything that I had to get done. But on the other hand, I couldn't seem to make any progress on my lists when I was awake, either. I tried switching to my family to-do notepad, which is where I keep birthday reminders. I thought to myself, 'What better way than to start with something I love to do?' I figured that if I could just get moving on *something*, if I could cross *just one thing* off my list, I would end my frustrating stint in to-do purgatory. But I found that I wasn't even capable of being a good birthday genie; toys were nothing but an indistinguishable blur as I scrolled through toy store Web sites trying to pick out a fun gift for my nephew, Logan. Worse, I couldn't think of anything pithy to say on the card for my closest friend from business school. After thirty minutes, I gave up and crawled back in bed."

Sleep evaded her and her tossing and turning ultimately

disturbed her husband's sleep as well. She explained why she couldn't sleep—an endless list for both work and family, and all attempts to accomplish anything were futile. Then he said something that ultimately created Button 2.

"He asked me to think about everything that was on my mind and pretend that I only had time to do three of the things on my list. Just three. I replied, 'Okay, but what does that have to do with anything? We're talking about all stuff that just has to get done. There is no option of only doing three things.' 'Well,' he asked, 'remember Pareto? The reality is that, yes, you can just do a small amount of things to take care of most of what is driving you crazy.'"

Understanding Pareto's Principle

The Pareto Principle, otherwise known as the 80/20 rule or the law of the vital few, basically states that in any pursuit, 80 percent of the consequences stem from 20 percent of the causes. Pareto was an Italian economist who came up with the 80/20 rule in 1906, observing that 80 percent of the wealth in Italy was owned by 20 percent of the Italian population.

Alicia knew from years of business experience what a great rule it was. Using Pareto's Principle had helped her as a marketer a number of times. Most memorably, she had been part of a team charged with turning around a national brand that had stalled. The small, three-person team was given a very limited marketing budget and had to deliver results in twelve months. The deck was stacked against them.

The only way to succeed was to focus on a small handful of initiatives that would likely have an outsized impact on the business. They started by identifying the markets that mattered most. Analysis showed roughly 20 percent of the markets in the United States accounted for nearly 75 percent of sales. The team chose to focus on driving the business in those markets only. If consumers in those markets purchased the product one more time per year, the business would be back on track.

Once the group had identified the priority markets, they had to figure out which marketing efforts would be most likely to help them reach their sales goal. The marketing budget could only realistically support two initiatives, but with fifteen on the table, the team had to choose the two that they believed would stretch their limited funds the farthest. Focus area one was a packaging redesign that made the product more noticeable on the supermarket shelf. Focus area two was local radio advertising that enabled the team to work extensively with local stations to promote the product during key drive times, and via contests and in-store promotions with the radio hosts.

The focus paid off. Within twelve months the business had stabilized. Had the marketers tried to do it all, they would have spun their wheels and gotten stuck, much like Alicia was that morning.

The way to apply the Pareto Principle to any to-do list is to go through the list and identify the 20 percent of the items that are crucial for moving forward and achieving larger goals. If you focus on fewer tasks, you have a better chance of completing them.

Scientific studies also back up the wisdom of focusing on fewer tasks. More of a focus means less of a tendency to multitask and less of a tendency to split your attention. According to a study in the *Journal of Experimental Psychology*,[2] people who multitask are less efficient than those who focus on one project at a time. The more complex the task, the more time you lose each time you switch back and forth among the tasks.

Paralysis in the face of endless lists and the struggle to let go of the less critical things on the list is pretty universal. In our conversations with hundreds of women across the United States over the past few years, we heard many similar stories. One thing is for certain: we all have lists that seem to be getting longer by the day. Sometimes they're written down (65 percent of the women we've spoken with write down their lists[3]) and sometimes we carry our to-do's around in our heads. Some days we are able to cross everything off the list, but on most days that just isn't possible.

The good news about Pareto's idea is that it doesn't require learning a complicated technique. Adapting the 80/20 rule to your lists simply means shifting the way you think about what you choose to do during the day. Focus on what you *can* do and *need* to do, let go (for now) of what you can't. It may sound simple, but if you've ever tried to consciously change even a small routine, like taking a detour on your drive home from work or parting your hair differently, you know how change doesn't seem to come naturally. It takes some focus and dedication to shift the way you've been doing things. However, once you start to integrate a change into your life, we know you'll feel a profound difference. Remember, it can take as little as two weeks to integrate a change into your life if you are determined to do so.

The great thing about choosing priorities is that it can help alleviate the background stress and uncomfortable feelings about what you're *not* doing. Not only will you get things done, your stress levels will decrease. Stress reduction doesn't just feel good; it can pay off big in dollar savings. The Centers for Disease Control and Prevention has reported that 80 percent of our medical expenditures are now stress related. The Pareto Principle can improve your health as well as help tackle your to-do list!

Organizational Inertia

If you're currently in a disorganized state, you are likely to stay there unless you can get momentum working in your favor. The trick: do one small thing that you can cross off of your organizational list. The simple act of completing an organizational task, no matter how small, gets the magic of momentum working for you, not against you! Although you've heard it a million times before, it's true that a series of small steps add up to real progress.

How to Choose Your Own Priorities

Choosing your own priorities might be an easy, off-the-top-of-the-head, no-brainer for you, or it might require a more formal process, like ranking all the items on your to-do list in the order of their importance. No matter which method works best for you, taking whatever time you need to determine essentials on your list is time well spent.

It is possible prioritizing is something you're doing already, in some way. The vast majority of women (90 percent) we spoke with have told us that they're confident in their ability to discern what's important to get done and to let go of what can't be done. However, in the rush of day-to-day life, squeaky wheels, unexpected "fire drills," and others' agendas often compete with our own priorities. Before you know it, you spend more of your limited time addressing things that aren't in line with your priorities.

Put the Big Picture on Your Lists

The "big picture" is central to the notion of setting priorities. The big picture comprises your short- and long-term goals: personal, professional, family, etc. It is easy to lose sight of them in the everyday swirl unless you make a conscious effort to map your to-do lists according to them. If your children, your aging mother, and your dog are your priorities, then you need to read through your to-do lists and bring to the top the items that have a direct impact on those three areas of your life. Everyone's global priorities will be different—but reading your lists with these filters applied will help you determine where to best put your energies to get the results you want.

Our friend Amy Keroes eloquently summarized the need to make the big picture part of your lists. "It's very easy to push important things off the list in the heat of the moment, especially if nobody is whining at you to do it. All too often, the proverbial squeaky wheel gets the grease in my life, not always the most critical or important wheel to focus on. When that happens, it also means that 'me time' is totally off the list (I certainly don't squeak at myself!)."

We suggest that you do two things to integrate the big picture with your lists.

First, write down your priorities at the top of your weekly to-do list and ideally at the top of any daily ones you keep too. Writing them down not only cements your commitment to them, but it makes it much easier to prioritize your lists. Check your lists for any tasks related to these goals and bring them to the top of your to-do list. If you don't have any tasks related to them on your list, put some down! It is easy to push big ticket or longer-term goals off the list because they appear to require more energy and time. But in reality, those bigger goals are simply achieved by taking a series of small steps every day. Consider what manageable tasks you can do today or this week to make progress against that goal.

Second, get in the habit of checking any new request that comes in against your priorities *before* you do it. This will give you a structure that enables you to table the nonessentials as they pop up.

Consider It . . . Not Done

As you cull through your lists, think about the consequences to the big picture if a particular task *didn't* get done. If you didn't organize that junk pile on your desk today, would you miss some bills that have to be paid by tomorrow and incur serious late fees? Would that ding your credit score and harm your chances of getting your dream house? If you didn't get little Harry's after-school commitments entered into your master calendar, would you likely over-schedule and miss important dates? Would you feel like a better mom if you were able to tell Harry in advance which events you would definitely be able to attend, and stick to it? If the implications of not getting something organized will have a negative impact on who you want to be and where you want to go, it counts as part of the 20 percent.

An additional gut check doesn't hurt. Think about how you'd *feel* if it didn't get done. If you feel anxious, notice your heart pumping faster or a slight queasiness in your stomach at the thought, chances are the task in question is a high priority.

Talk to Others

Another way to clarify your priorities is to remember that no woman is an island. You are part of a complex network of people, including your spouse and children, your siblings and parents, and your coworkers. It's good to communicate your priorities to those important people in your life and get a sense of their priorities as well. You may be surprised to learn you aren't necessarily on the same page. When you're not in sync, there is a higher likelihood that you will end up with conflicts and/or be put in situations that make it difficult to stick to a plan.

Irina Baranov, wife, mother, daughter, sister, granddaughter, friend, and marketing director for the nonprofit Council for Relationships in Philadelphia, manages to keep her hectic life on track using an inventive (and fun!) combination of these techniques. Approximately once a quarter, she and her husband schedule an "off-site" meeting to discuss their joint, individual, and family priorities. They arrange for one of their parents to watch their kids for the weekend and then head to a relaxing spot. During the course of the weekend they talk about the state of their current life and dream about their future. Everything is covered, from their children's education to their daily grind, from monthly budgets to retirement plans. "When we first started doing these, we followed a more formal list," she says. "But now that we've got the hang of it, the conversations are very free-form and they just sort of ebb and flow over meals and throughout the weekend." By the end of two days, they both leave with a very clear sense of their overall priorities, not to mention a renewed connection and recharged batteries.

Then when it comes to keeping those priorities day-to-day, Irina reviews her to-do lists, making sure that her everyday priorities are in line with the ones she and her husband agreed to. She rank orders her list and puts the most critical three, four, or five tasks at the top. Then she makes sure her schedule can accommodate those priorities. If a task requires focus and quiet, such as writing a presentation, she'll schedule a meeting with herself so that she can turn off the phones, shut the door, and get the important work done. If she sees a high-priority task on her list that she doesn't like to do, she will make it the top priority and force herself to do it first thing.

Prepare for the Unexpected

A top 20 percent priority that is universally applicable is planning ahead for how your family would cope in the face of a

Pinch Points Can Pinpoint Your Priorities

If you find yourself struggling to organize your list, "pinch points" are another useful way to identify priorities. If you ever had a grandmother pinch your cheeks as a child, you know that sore, uncomfortable tight feeling. Or, have you ever turned on a garden hose and then pinched off the flow by stepping on it? The pressure will build behind the pinch point until the hose stretches—or bursts. In life it's the same thing: pinch points are places where something—maybe the stacks of mail and bills or the way you keep your family calendar—acts like a pinched valve, backing up other important things, making you feel uncomfortable, stressed, and stretched. That feeling of discomfort over a particular area and how it is (or isn't) organized is your cue that something needs to be done. Pinch points are areas you need to pay attention to in order to feel organized.

natural disaster or other unexpected emergency. Sure, a disaster is probably not going to strike you tomorrow, but disasters aren't action items you can put on the calendar. Logically, it's best to assume that they may happen tomorrow, and be ready for them.

The best news about being prepared is that there may be some positive side effects on your day-to-day organization as well. First, that low-level anxiety that you carry around because you know you aren't prepared will disappear. Second, you won't waste time searching for important documents like medical records and insurance policies because you'll know exactly where they are located. Set it and forget it.

The Nonessentials

If you understand how to prioritize, but feel yourself resisting the idea that you must choose among your long lists of to-do's, you might be concerned about what items will get left behind. You may be saying to yourself, "Will my bedroom get painted, will my lawn mower get fixed, will my holiday cards get written, and will I get to go to the gym if that to-do doesn't make it into my top priorities?"

We want to be clear that just because a task on your list isn't a top priority doesn't mean you should give up on it altogether. The 80/20 rule is intended to help you focus on the most important tasks, so that those definitely get crossed off the list. It is also a method for letting go of the guilt, anxiety, and inertia that comes along with a to-do list that has more tasks on it than you have time to accomplish. By all means, if you have enough time to tackle additional items once you've crossed the priorities off your list—hop to it!

Emergency Preparedness—a Top 20 Percent Priority for Everyone

Why is it that the only time we think to get prepared is when disaster is breathing down our necks? So often we hear about hurricanes, fires, or other disasters and think, "I should really put a few things together in case of an emergency," but never actually get around to doing so. It's a universal problem driven by two big fears. First, for many of us, it's difficult to be sure what is needed or how to put it together. Second, the thought of something bad happening to us or our loved ones is often too difficult to consider so our denial leaves us immobilized. These are fears worth overcoming because the benefits of being prepared are twofold—you'll be set in the event of a disaster and you'll no longer have that little voice in the back of your mind nagging you to take the action. The most important step in getting prepared is to be informed. There are many Web sites that can help you wrap your head around what exactly you need to get ready for anything. One of the best Web sites is by the Department of Homeland Security at www.ready.gov. The site walks you through what you'll need to be prepared in an emergency, including:

- Assembling an emergency supply kit—what are the necessary items or essentials of survival: water, food, clean air, and warmth.

- Making an emergency plan—what are the important components of a plan? Keeping informed and connected— where should you look for important directives and how to be sure family members can contact one another.

The truth is: if you decide it needs to get done, it will get done. Here's the way we see the process working: You pick your own priorities. And they can change as you see fit—they can be for the month, for the week, or for the day. You decide.

Be open to the possibility that only those things on your priority list will definitely get crossed off today, and accept the fact that the others might not. If you notice that there is a task on your list that isn't a top priority, but you know someone else is expecting you to get it done, let them know it may not get done today. For example, if your husband asks you to help him pick out a birthday gift for his mother (whose birthday is tomorrow) and you know you have higher priorities to take care of today, let him know. It doesn't have to be negative. "Honey, I'd love to help you, but I don't see how I can get it done today. I've got car pool duty morning and afternoon, I have to whip up a costume for Jenny's play, pay the bills, and meet my mom at the heart specialist at lunch. Your mom is going to visit her friend in Maine next week, why don't you get her something for that trip?"

Trust that your non-priority to-do's can get prioritized into tomorrow's list, or next week's, or next month's. This isn't procrastination; it's fitting a reasonable number of tasks into a reasonable amount of time, and allowing the spillover to fit into a different slot of time. You can't do it all at once and if you pick and choose what will get done in a certain time frame you're much more likely to be efficient and effective. Also, delegating or sharing to-do's is an option, which we will discuss in the next chapter.

For Alicia, a non-priority is hanging pictures in her house. "I just accept the fact that it's going to happen eventually, but slower than a lot of other things in my life." If you can accept—and trust—that your non-priorities will get done on a schedule that is appropriate for them, you'll find the process of setting priorities much smoother.

Give 80/20 a Try

Here are two simple exercises we recommend to help you identify your own critical 20 percent. There are no hard-and-fast rules here. These exercises are less about learning a new technique than they are about practice in learning a new philosophy, or a new way of thinking. Each exercise takes less than thirty minutes to complete. At the end of the exercise, you will be left with a short list of items you can focus on. Hopefully, you will have gained the ability to let go of the rest. You might find the exercises a challenge or you might find them fun, but either way we know you'll find them useful!

The One-Hour Rule

This exercise is a good one to try if you need help determining the most important tasks to focus on. You can try this exercise silently on your own, or out loud with a friend or a loved one you trust. Doing it with someone may make it more fun and they may even give you some good insight on what really should be important.

1. Get out your latest to-do list and a blank sheet of paper. If you do not have a current to-do list, spend fifteen minutes writing down everything you want to get done this week. Make sure to include things for work, for the family, and for you. Include any deadlines for time-sensitive tasks.

2. On the blank sheet of paper, write down your "big picture" goals at the top. If you have not articulated them, take ten minutes to consider the things you really want to accomplish in these areas: you (personal growth and development), your job, your health, your family, your friends, and your finances.

3. Now, take your to-do list and imagine that you only have one hour over the next week to get things done. One hour. What are the handful of tasks that you would have to focus on? Circle those items. Keep in mind that just because something has a deadline doesn't necessarily mean it is a priority. Be sure that you weigh each task against your big picture goals.

4. Imagine that you magically found one more hour this week to do things. What are the additional things you would focus on? Put a circle around those as well.

What you have now is a short list that will most likely cover your critical 20 percent. Look closely at this shortened list and pay attention to how you feel now and how you think you would feel if you only got these items done, and nothing else, for the next week. If you are like most of us, you will probably feel a little uncomfortable. We did when we first started. Try it, though, and soon you will see how easy it is to pick the 20 percent and let the rest go. Remember that just because something doesn't get done this week it doesn't mean it won't ever get done. You are making a realistic list that sets you up for success rather than failure.

What You Write Down Gets Done

The next exercise is designed to get you moving and crossing things off that list! Look at the priorities you identified in the last exercise, the One-Hour Rule. Assign to each priority one or more of the following possible categories:

Just me—I have total control over this task.

Not mine—If you can't have complete control, who is the main person or persons responsible for this issue? Be specific.

Fight—Is this an issue that causes tension in the household?

Mark your priorities quickly, without too much thought. Remember, there are no right or wrong answers here.

Take a closer look at the items and the categories you assigned to them. The categories are designed to help you figure out how to keep momentum working in your favor as you start to tackle those priorities.

Just me—These are the issues on the list that you have total power over. To keep things moving in the right direction, intersperse these tasks with those that are not in your control and/or that cause tension in the household. Just-me tasks are also a natural place to start.

Not mine—These are the issues on your list that you influence, but do not control. Examples are: your husband needs to pay the contractor before you can schedule a final inspection for a basement renovation or your daughter needs to get the exact dates of her upcoming class trip to D.C. so you and your husband can schedule a dinner party.

Rather than simply keeping a list of the end task and hoping that it will get crossed off, list next to the task logical check-in points with the person or people who have control over the task. Then schedule check-in points—phone calls, reminder e-mails, or in-person chats. That is something you can do right now to make sure everyone is on track.

Fight—These are the issues on your list that require discussion and may often spark a fight. They can include things like paying the bills or scheduling who will cover the next three 7:00 A.M. Saturday soccer games. Conflict isn't enjoyable, and many people have a tendency to shy away from tasks that engender it. Know that it's best not to handle a potentially stressful interaction when you or the person you have to interact with is tired, grumpy, hungry, rushed, or you haven't practiced what you *want* to say and what you *won't* say! Be thoughtful and schedule such tasks in windows that are least likely to spark a fight.

Hopefully, this chapter has helped you think through which tasks are most critical for you to complete and which projects you can consider putting aside or letting go. It is important to remember that the only person who can determine what is most important to get Buttoned Up is you. Everyone has a different set of priorities, issues, and wishes. It is also important to revisit these critical items frequently because over time, just as life changes, these will certainly change too.

Button 2: You Don't Have to Do Everything on Your List

Use the Pareto Principle to identify the 20 percent of the items that are crucial for you moving forward. If you focus on fewer tasks, you have a better chance at completing them.

Focus on what you can do and need to do and let go (for now) of what you can't. Remember that it takes some focus and dedication to shift the way you've been doing things.

To Evaluate Your Lists and Identify Priorities:

1. **Keep the big picture close by**—Write your goals at the top of your to-do lists.

2. **Consider it not done**—Think about the consequences if the task isn't completed. Could it be dangerous to your health, your family, your job, your home, your financial well-being?

3. **Communicate with others, and make sure you're in sync.**

Let go of anything not on your priority list and accept the fact that it won't get done today. This isn't procrastination. It's fitting a reasonable number of tasks into a reasonable amount of time and setting yourself up for successes rather than failure.

You Don't Need to Do Everything Yourself

B uttoned Up secret #3: "You don't need to do everything yourself" may sound liberating and puzzling all at once. You might be asking yourself, "If I don't do it, who will?" Admittedly, delegating is a challenge, but it's also a very learnable skill with a sweet payoff.

Does My Baby Really Care Who Buys His Diapers?

How can you determine if you're not trying to do everything yourself when you shouldn't be? Sarah's aha moment came the day she brought her first child, William, home from the hospital on a warm Sunday morning in the summer of 2006. She and her husband, Gardiner, had done what they thought was a thorough job of setting up the nursery. They had a crib, changing table, diapers, clothes, soaps, lotions, a thermometer, toys, blankets—the works. But they were in for a rude awakening.

Because their son Will was on the small side, they found that the diapers they purchased came up to his chin. Then they realized they had no diaper ointment. Then they realized they had no diaper pail, no soft little cotton pads to wipe his little bottom, and no plastic bowl to put warm water in for wetting the soft little cotton pads that they didn't have. Then they realized that not only didn't they have enough bottles, but the ones they did have didn't have the right nipples. Will got too much milk too fast. Then they realized they didn't have a pacifier. The list of forgotten or never considered items went on and on! Sarah felt like a complete failure (already!) as a mom, for missing such obvious things. Sarah also realized that she and Gar were failing as a team, because they weren't getting the important things done.

Sarah felt she had to compensate for her perceived failure by going out and getting all the supplies herself. She refused to let her husband go by himself to the store with a list to get what they needed for a properly stocked nursery. She piled everyone into the car and sped to the nearest CVS and then on to the grocery store. Sarah felt resentment toward Gar because she was doing more, even though she insisted on going to the store herself. After two hours of shopping, Sarah was exhausted, the baby was crying for his next feeding, and her usually gentle husband, Gar, was growling at her because she was acting like such a neurotic control freak. It wasn't until they were waiting for the light to change at a stoplight that she took a moment to breathe and realized that she was acting like a crazy woman.

Postpartum brain, guilt, inner control freak—no matter what was driving Sarah to overcorrect her mistake and take charge, we've probably all been there. We've all felt that if we do it ourselves it will get done better, faster, or more perfectly. Letting go of the "if you want it done right, do it yourself" dictum can not only open you up, but let you get more done.

Warning Signs that You Need to Delegate

Have you felt your internal warning signs—that uncomfortable, anxious, squirmy, got-to-look-at-my-watch-every-second feeling? The feeling that no one around you, including you, is very happy whatever you do? That's the sign that there's got to be a better way. In a clear thinking moment, at that stoplight, Sarah vowed to get it together.

The key was to enlist the aid of her husband to raise awareness of when she needed help. When she talked it over with Gar, he asked her how she might remember this insight in the heat of some future battle. They decided to try out an "early warning system" that would alert them when Sarah was overstretched and could let go of something.

Sarah's early warning sign number one: the alarm clock. Setting it earlier and earlier so that you have time to cross everything off your list and still try to get some semblance of exercise three days a week is a signal that you need to delegate something or a few things. Sign number two: dropping a ball, like forgetting to book a babysitter for a Saturday night date or paying a bill a day late. Finally, sign number three: the crab factor. When you're stressed out and a little short with people or cranky for more than a few hours, it's a sign you've got too much on your plate and something has to give.

If the benefits of delegating are substantial, the hazards of trying to do it all yourself are equally so. The most common side effect of carrying too big a load is burnout. According to clinical psychologists, burnout is a physical, mental, and emotional response to constant levels of high stress.[1] Not only does it feel awful (it produces feelings of hopelessness, powerlessness, cynicism, resentment, and failure), but it also makes you less productive and prone to stagnation.

Why Women Don't Easily Delegate

At work, delegating is a fact of life for women managers like Alicia, who delegated to staffs as large as twenty for over fifteen years. Employees expect a boss to assign them new tasks and to guide them in getting them done, with the ultimate goal of making the organization work. An uncooperative employee can lose his or her job. A willing employee can get rewarded with more money and a promotion. "You don't have to love me," a boss may whisper under her breath, "just get the job done." Clearly women have the skills and ability that allow them to delegate to others. When they are out of the office, it's a different story.

The Math of Leverage

Consider this: if you were able to assign to another person one or two tasks that collectively consumed fifteen minutes a day, you would gain an extra ninety-one hours a year! On a more modest scale, that means you'd gain an extra one hour, forty-five minutes *per week*. How might you use that extra time to do something you really want or need to do?

When that same woman walks in the door of her own home, her paycheck, relative to her husband's, may change the playing field. The amount of money a woman makes outside of the home can really affect the balance of power inside the home. Although the yearly value of an average woman's housework is at least $25,000, a woman earning less income than her husband may think, "What right do I have to delegate?" when requesting family members help with the housework. Women who are stay-at-home moms with no salary share this feeling as well. A woman may question whether she should delegate tasks to her husband who is working at an office all day because she feels guilty about not getting "her" job done as well as not contributing financially to the family. There are other reasons that women tend to think we can do it ourselves:

The person I want to delegate to may say no or get angry: When it comes to parental urgings to clean their room, some kids "just say no." Husbands also may not jump up and down with joy at the opportunity to do the dishes. There are options here, which will be discussed in depth later, but negotiation is key. You and your spouse may decide to achieve balance and try to keep your household contributions even. Incentives can also work. Offer a carrot like getting to choose the movie on Saturday night or getting to sleep in on Sunday morning when trying to persuade your partner to take on a task or responsibility that will lighten your load.

I fear that it won't be done right or that others will judge unless I do it myself: Sometimes there's a compulsion to do it yourself and do it perfectly. Many women have perfectionist tendencies, and tend to go into an "I can do it all" frenzy when they fear others might see what a mess they actually are on the inside. Somehow "controlling" little details in moments of chaos helps them to ignore how out of line they might be with the bigger picture. Doing it all is also a way to try to assuage the guilt that comes from living a life that does not necessarily fit into a traditional mold. If you're a CEO or a stay-at-home mom, *not* doing something that's traditionally mom territory can open you up to criticism from others—or yourself.

There may be an area of the home—laundry, bills, grocery shopping—that you feel you have down to an art form and if it's not done to your standard it may as well not be done at all. This is that yardstick issue again. It's hard to let go of something you do really well, but it can be a necessity if you are overburdened and stressed by your responsibilities.

If you think about ditching perfection, you'll have a good start to letting go of this barrier to delegating.

Money is a problem: There are two sides to the coin here. It's hard to enlist the willing assistance of family members or outsiders when you don't have money to pay for services, or if you're feeling that your lack of a salaried job gives you no leverage when asking for help. On the flip side, it can be equally difficult paying an outsider to do the job that family members have the skills to complete. Don't get stuck in this dilemma. Delegating and negotiating—with or without monetary payment—can help you overcome this problem.

If it comes down to paying someone, remember, we all make choices about how we spend our money. For example, would you rather take one family trip to Disney World—for, say, $5,000—or take that amount and spend $100 every week to get help with your chores so you have two or three more free hours each week to spend with your family? It comes down to prioritizing over the long term to decide how best to spend your time and money. You don't have to break the bank to get extra help with chores or babysitting. Some employees who give excellent value for money include high school students, college students, and live-in au pairs who receive room and board in exchange for child care.

It takes too long to give the job to someone else: Teaching someone else how to handle a household responsibility can be a useful, productive activity when you look at it as mentoring or nurturing another person. Repetitive tasks are often more appropriate and more easily delegated, and on those tasks the time spent teaching can be shared over a number of repetitions. As a starting point, try dividing up the task at hand. For example, you wash, I'll dry.

I like doing this: Deb likes folding shirts. Hannah likes paying the bills. You may have a particular chore that you think, "It's not so bad." Admittedly, fun chores are usually delegated less often than uninteresting (e.g., house-cleaning) or frustratingly complex ones (e.g., doing the taxes). Try to keep the end goal in mind. The end goal of delegating is to off-load some items from your plate that can be accomplished by someone else so that you have time to do the thing only you *can* do or *want* to do (e.g., snuggle with your daughter). Don't forget that delegating doesn't have to be an all-or-nothing proposition—you can delegate when you need to, on a case by case basis. Delegating can also be sharing a responsibility. This way with more people working on the task, the job will get done faster—and leave you more time for snuggling with your child, or doing what you want to do.

How to Pick a Task to Delegate and
Who to Delegate It To

Before you actually jump in the delegating pool, check out the waters by sitting along the side and considering your options. Use them to help you plan your delegations at home:

1. **Who has an incentive to get the job done?** (The more the incentive, the more likely someone is to get it done!) Family members can be motivated to complete tasks by positive reinforcement through encouragement and material rewards. One busy mom we know encourages her daughter to sleep in her room and make her own bed by using a sticker card. Every morning that she sleeps in her own bed and makes it, she gets a sticker to put on a card. After five days with consecutive stickers, her daughter receives a reasonable present, like a special bike ride with Mom and Dad or a new outfit for her favorite doll. Incentives help people reach long-term goals as well as help with delegating.

2. **Who has the skills to do the task?** (It's best if the person already has the skills, or you to have the time to enjoy teaching them the skills.)

3. **Is the task repetitive in nature?** (Repetitive tasks are easier to delegate because they offer more opportunities to see the task done correctly.)

4. **Is there room for error?** (Tasks that don't have to be accomplished in a very specific way are great to delegate, because you can let a person get the task done their way, as long as it meets your objectives.)

If you delegate doing the dishes and the dishes are clean, you don't have to worry. Even if your husband or child loaded the dishwasher in a different way, ran a different rinse cycle, or didn't close the soap cap, the important thing to remember is that the task is done!

Once you have targeted your task, determined the best person for the job, and decided for yourself the margin of error you can live with, it's time to get delegating.

Nine Steps in the Delegating Dance

Effective delegation is not telling someone exactly how to do something step-by-step and then standing over them while it gets done. It is also not handing a job over to a person and walking away entirely. Effective delegation involves a series of steps that allow you to cross something off of your list and hand it over to someone else who will accomplish a specific task (or tasks) in a specific time frame. Delegation isn't pushing something unwanted onto another person—it's actually a true example of teamwork.

Let's go back to the dishwashing example and see how you can effectively delegate this task and ensure a desirable outcome. Let's say you want help in getting the dishes done. As you read through each step, imagine how you would enact it with your family member or situation.

Step 1: Determine your desired outcome. Articulate to yourself the desired outcome of the task you want accomplished. In this case, the outcome is pretty simple: clean, shiny dishes with no remnants of food. To make your expectations abundantly clear, put a completion time on it that you'd like as well—for example, "I would like to have the dinner dishes clean by the following morning."

Before you approach someone else to do the task, you may find it helpful to be clear on why you want to delegate it. What will you gain by delegating? What will happen if it doesn't get delegated? Come up with a plan B before you start so you can comfortably negotiate without anger or desperation if you meet any reluctance from the person you're asking to do the task. But be clear: plan B does not simply mean throwing your hands in the air and doing the task yourself. You may have to talk with the person you asked to complete the task to resolve the problem. If you take over, the lesson they learn is: why bother, she's just going to do it her way anyway. Effective delegation won't come perfectly at first, and it is something you will need to work on.

Step 2: Select the person who can best help you accomplish this task. Make a list of all of the possible people you can delegate to. Think about who has the time, best skills, and willingness to get this job done. For example, you might choose to ask your husband to do the dishes each night after dinner. Or alternatively, if you have older children, they might be perfectly capable (though, of course, not always willing—that's where the discussion comes in) of doing this task too. The discussion can center around expectations you have of your older child in terms of what you ask them to do around the house. Tell your spouse or child why they are best for the task and they will feel a greater responsibility to complete the task. You can negotiate by offering incentives if they help complete chores for a certain number of days in a row—for example, if the whole family helps out consistently for a month, everyone will be rewarded with a family vacation.

Step 3: Get an agreement from that person to listen. Ask your chosen person for five or ten minutes to talk to them about the task at hand.

Step 4: Give the person important context. Talk to the person you want to delegate to about why this is important, why you need help, and why you think they, in particular, are the best person for the job. For example, set aside five minutes with your husband to talk about why it is hard after working all day to both make dinner and then clean up. Also, you can say that doing these things prevents you from having sufficient time with the kids before they go to bed.

Step 5: Be specific about what you need and when you need it. Give the person who you are delegating to all of the specifics of the project. This includes: objective, timing, description of the task, criteria for success. For dishwashing, you would want the dishes done and dishwasher run every night after dinner. The criterion for success would be clean dishes ready to use for breakfast by the next morning.

Step 6: Negotiate so that the task works for both people. Try to make sure everyone has something to gain by sharing the burden of the task. For example, if Dad does the dishes each night, Mom will make dinner and then get the kids ready to go to bed. This step ensures give-and-take and that both parties agree on who will do what and when it will be done. You can negotiate that Dad only does the dishes during the workweek, and Mom or the kids will handle the weekend dishes while Dad plays golf or watches his favorite sports shows.

Step 7: Clarify your agreement. Once you have negotiated who will do what, make sure you repeat your agreement on tasks. This should include not just the task to be done but the parameters around the task as well. For example, the dishes will get done by Dad each weeknight after dinner. While this is being done, Mom will get the kids ready for bed. If Dad gets home late or has work to do, he will talk to Mom about her doing the dishes for that one specific night. Delegations, especially a system like Dad doing the dishes each weeknight, should be permanent so your family takes the tasks and responsibilities seriously. But if the system of delegation isn't working out for your family needs, you will have to revisit the issue and make changes.

Step 8: Step back and let the person do the task at hand. Don't criticize or watch over the task being done. Accept that the task will not be done exactly the way you would do it but recognize that as long as it is accomplished and done on time, that it is okay. If the dishes are clean the next morning, do not worry about how they were loaded in the dishwasher or if they were rinsed off first. Accepting imperfection and letting go are keys to successful delegation.

Step 9: Last but not least, provide feedback, especially positive feedback. Once the task has been completed, give constructive feedback to the person. As a guideline, tell the person five great things about the job for every one criticism. "Honey, you did a great job with the dishes. It took a lot of pressure off of me and I really appreciate it. I could not believe how great it was to come into the kitchen in the morning and have the dishes all done. Thank you. One thing—it would be great if you would try to put the wineglasses on the top shelf of the dishwasher so we can avoid them breaking. Thanks again."

Choosing What to Delegate

Now you are ready to try an exercise that will help you pick a task to delegate. First, make a list of the tasks you currently do that you would like help with. Limit your list to a maximum of twenty tasks. You might want to include household chores like setting and clearing the table, vacuuming, or home management chores like bill paying and doing taxes. Also include less frequent tasks like closet cleaning and washing and waxing the cars. Once you have this list, apply our 80/20 rule to determine what tasks to delegate. It is really very simple. Keep 20 percent of the list for you. Those items are probably things you do not feel comfortable delegating or that may require too much of your own time to manage someone else doing it to be worth your while. With the remaining 80 percent, you have two choices: delegate the task, or stop doing it. We find this exercise is one of the best ways to force someone to delegate who does not like to give up control of things. Try it. You have nothing to lose and only free time to gain.

Epiphany

Delegating buys you time; the time you need to complete the most pressing tasks or just to have "you time." This BU Time allows you to pay attention to the things that really matter. Waiting in line in the grocery store may be something you'll give up to be able to snuggle on the couch with your child, read a book, exercise or do any other activity you value. Your free time may also give you an opportunity to rethink how you want to be spending your time altogether.

Alicia and Sarah used delegation to free up the time they needed to nurture a dream they had to create Buttoned Up, Inc., and the book you're reading right now!

Button 3: You Don't Need to Do Everything Yourself

Warning signs that you may need to delegate are: you're getting up earlier or staying up later to get it all done, you drop the ball, or you're feeling stressed and cranky.

To pick a task to delegate and the person to delegate it to, find the person with the incentive and skills to get the job done. The best tasks to delegate are repetitive and have room for error.

Nine Steps to Delegating:

1. Determine your desired outcome.

2. Select the person who can best help you accomplish this task.

3. Get agreement from that person to listen.

4. Give the person important context.

5. Be specific about what you need and when you need it.

6. Negotiate so that the task works for both people.

7. Clarify your agreement.

8. Step back and let the person do the task at hand.

9. Provide positive feedback.

Pick a Room and Get Started

n Sarah's sunny yellow kitchen is a weathered pine table that became the repository of all papers, bills, catalogs, and more. That table became a symbol of disorganization for Sarah and the more the paper piled up the less able she felt to tackle and master the piles.

Sarah vs. the Kitchen Table

Most people have a room in their home that whimpers or roars "help me" because of the way it looks and works, or doesn't work. Each week you vow to finally organize that one space but it always seems too large to resolve. Left on its own, it is the room that causes the most anxiety and stress. Everyone has that room, or area in a room. For Sarah, that room is the kitchen and the kitchen table in particular. She usually enters her home after work weighted down with her laptop in a shoulder bag, groceries, a handful of toys, and her son's backpack. There's a mail slot in the door, which means she can only open the door a slit and then has to juggle everything as she stoops to pick up the pile of bills, magazines, and junk dropped through the slot by the mailman earlier in the day that now lies scattered all over the floor. The first piece of furniture she encounters after getting through the door is the kitchen table, so everything in her arms gets joyously and unceremoniously dumped onto the table to be dealt with later. Unfortunately, later never seems to come.

In the post-work rush of getting dinner for her family, getting her son to bed, and taking a little time to decompress from a hectic workday, the piles on the table are left unattended—sometimes for days at a time. So the stack of stuff remains. And the cycle repeats itself again each night. More mail unceremoniously dumped on the table. It's not uncommon for piles that were semi-organized into logical groups on Monday to slide into one giant, amorphous, listing heap by Thursday. Packages, boxes, newspapers, and other bulkier items often spread like weeds to the nearby window seat.

Because these piles have become such a fact of life, Sarah's husband nicknamed them "craplet piles." While it helps that they have a sense of humor about it, even that silly word said with a French accent (*zee craplets on zee table*) can't mask the energy-sapping effect the piles have on both of them. As with anything left undone, such piles can make anyone feel disorganized and fearful that something important will be lost in the shuffle. It might not inspire a full-bore panic but can lead to constant low-level stress, tension, anxiety, and headaches.

Because your particular stress-inducing situation might be different from Sarah's, your solutions will also be different, but it will be instructive to see how she coped—and how you might be able to adapt her coping methods to your home.

"We were motivated to make this kitchen work because the

stress-causing piles made us angry, tense, and started us fighting. My husband is a 'saver.' I'm a 'tosser.' He's saving an article on strengthening his abs from a men's health magazine that he hasn't looked at since he ripped it out. I've swept whole, never-looked-at piles into the trash in a fit of frustration—piles that included bills and checks for my husband, who's an independent film editor. We knew we had a problem. We knew how it made us feel. Fortunately, we also knew we were not alone."

That stack of "stuff" lurking in the corner, spread out across the table, or even collecting dust in an overstuffed box in the corner takes an emotional toll. Psychological researchers have found that a constant barrage of physical and informational clutter leads to higher levels of cardiovascular stress, impaired judgment, and a noticeable drop in civility to others. We've heard hundreds of women across America tell us through e-mail and mall surveys that their ongoing battles with clutter made them "anxious" and "stressed-out."

Take a mental walk around your own home to pinpoint your own trouble spot. If it doesn't immediately jump out at you, simply close your eyes for a few seconds and mentally "feel" your way to that room. It's the room that makes you feel slightly tense when you think about it or even walk past. It's the room you slammed the door on before your mother-in-law came for a visit. It's the room that attracts and spawns clutter like a weed-filled garden.

The living room/family room, the kitchen, or the home office are the most common trouble spots. The trouble spots can also be specific areas of a room like your desk in your office, the cupboards in the playroom, or the table in the kitchen. But even if one area of the room is messy, it still causes you great stress and makes the whole room a trouble spot. The exact location may differ from household to household, as will the degree to which messiness is tolerated, but . . . we all have *that room.*

Calculating the Impact of Organizational Stress

Our friend Deb shared her formula for calculating the impact of different types of clutter in her life. She uses three variables to create a sort of "stress-o-meter" that helps her prioritize her organizational tasks.

The three variables:

General clutter: Anything you feel isn't in its proper place (papers, clothes, toys, and so on).

Visibility: The extent to which clutter is out in the open and likely to be seen by others.

MIAs: Items currently missing in action, and which you are certain are somewhere amidst the clutter (bills, insurance documents, field-trip permission slips, and more).

The more variables added to the clutter mix, and the higher their degree, the higher her level of stress and anxiety. Fortunately, there is a huge positive impact on her life if she addresses the clutter and gets it under control.

Making Change

There are changes or shifts in beliefs and behavior that you need to make before you can possibly de-clutter the room that is causing you trouble:

Change 1: It doesn't have to be perfect.

Change 2: Focus on what's important.

Change 3: Ask for help.

Change 1: It Doesn't Have to Be Perfect

Glossy decorating magazines are great for ideas. As we mentioned, we like to call them Org Porn because they present a larger unattainable ideal. Do they start you daydreaming about transforming your trouble spot into a pristine oasis fit for a photo shoot? Don't spin your wheels. Instead, be realistic about what constitutes "success" for this room. For any solution to work, it has to fit into your life, not vice versa. You can be inspired by these magazines, just don't let them rule your life.

"The first step in addressing our kitchen table problem was actually accepting the fact that it was always going to be a magnet for mail and a general dumping ground because of its location," said Sarah. "In that spirit, we had to let go of the fantasy that our table would be like those perfect red rose centerpiece tables in a glossy magazine." But, giving up perfect doesn't mean you throw in the towel entirely.

For something to be Buttoned Up, it doesn't have to be pristine. Being Buttoned Up is a confident, relaxed state of mind. It comes when you are able to identify and implement organizational solutions that will bend, stretch, and roll with life's little (and not so little) hiccups. Being Buttoned Up isn't a static end state. Rather, it's a framework you can use for absorbing the "stuff" of everyday life without losing your cool. It's adaptable to your current situation and needs.

Sarah summed up how chasing an unattainable ideal can cause you to get stuck. "We hadn't realized it, but our belief that a flawless table was a requirement for being 'organized' was keeping us from implementing some really simple ideas that would help us keep the mail and general clutter under control. Much like chasing model-thinness as the goal in your weight-loss program, trying to achieve and maintain immaculate spaces is also unrealistic and unattainable. We started by accepting our imperfect kitchen table. Ditching that need for perfection allowed us to find a few basic steps that led us, slowly but surely, to the organized kitchen we wanted."

Before you get carried away with the fantasy of perfection, take a moment to imagine the photo shoot for the red rose centerpiece table *before* the magazine photo was shot. There were days spent finding the perfect vase and the perfect flowers. There were stressful moments with the photographer yelling, "Who touched my table? Get me the Windex, quick!" But that's not real life; people actually *live* in your room. Because no one is perfect, your room can't be either. That's okay. It's not perfection we're focusing on here; we're focusing on what is important for you, your room, and your life.

Change 2: Focus on What's Important

When you're standing in the midst of your trouble spot, it is easy to feel the paralysis of the overwhelmed. Your eyes are drawn to things that say "put me away" and "deal with me now!" While everything in sight is clamoring for your attention, your brain kicks in and says, "I don't have time for this," or "Cleaning this up won't solve the problem because the piles will return." So you end up stuck, and probably feeling guilty about it.

It's easy to ignore a problem. Most people feel they have to either address the whole thing at once, or they shouldn't even try. Without action, most people try to ignore the problem—but that doesn't work, either. The problem becomes a constant reminder of the failure to get organized.

The best way we know how to get unstuck is to focus on a handful of problems. Then take action on those very few items right away. To get clarity on which tasks matter most, ask yourself three simple questions:

1. **General clutter—the visual aspect:** What two or three tasks would have the biggest impact on how I feel the room works?

2. **Visibility—the functional aspect:** What one or two tasks would have the biggest impact on how this room looked?

3. **The MIA motivators:** What are the two or three things that will come back to haunt me (such as a late fee, a missed event) if I don't deal with them now?

The answers to these questions will give you a list of two or three tasks per question, which will help you stay focused on those things that will really make the biggest difference. Don't worry about the rest. Get momentum working in your favor now by taking some action around those top priority tasks.

Two friends, Dustin and Katie, share a system they created for culling the "craplets." They realized the worst offender was junk mail, quickly followed by bills, and then by magazines or newspaper articles they wanted to save for one reason or another.

Dustin and Katie bought a stylish trash bin for paper recyclables that they put right next to the table. That's where all junk mail is now immediately tossed and then moved to the recycle bin once a week. Then they purchased a wooden mail depot with three bins that they hung on the wall adjacent to the kitchen entrance. All of Dustin's bills are placed in his bin, Katie's in her bin, and articles/magazines in the third bin. While they still have the occasional stray item lingering mischievously on their tabletop, they are able now to actually eat on their nice old barn plank table. The table is now getting used for its intended purpose and the mail, bills, and other papers are being handled effectively.

Change 3: Ask for Help

Once you are clear on what you need to do, ask for a little help in dealing with the problem area and maintaining it going forward. This is particularly important if the room is used by quite a number of people. In a recent survey conducted by Buttoned Up, we found that in nearly 75 percent of U.S. homes, the responsibility for organizing the house is shouldered by one person alone (and 68 percent of the time, it's by an already busy working mom).[1] Delegating effectively can be a tough challenge but it is one well worth overcoming. Consider this: enlisting the help of your "team" (spouse, children, roommates) will make all of you more efficient and happier. It can also mean more time for everyone to do the things they enjoy. Doing everything by yourself demoralizes others because it robs them of the opportunity to add value with their own creative approaches to getting work done. It can make you feel resentful that you are shouldering the burden of keeping the house in order. All in all, when one person takes on everything it can lead to unhappiness all around.

In order to delegate effectively, first ask yourself who the culprits of the disorganization actually are. Is it you? Is it your spouse? Is it both of you? If you have children, what about them? Chances are not only one person is responsible for the disorder. One thing is for sure: the room will never stay organized if you don't enlist the help of people who contribute to the disarray in the first place.

Sarah and Gardiner determined that they were largely responsible for the kitchen table chaos, and since Gardiner is a pack rat he may have had more responsibility for keeping the pile alive. Clearly they both needed to take action if they were going to get the piles in control, reclaim their kitchen table, and more effectively handle the mail, bills, etc.

Sarah and Gardiner's Plan

Sarah and Gar tackled their kitchen table problem by first purchasing a storage unit for their kitchen table clutter. The bins in the unit were delegated to bills, Sarah's mail, and Gar's mail. Once a night, before climbing the stairs to bed, they take the daily mini-pile from the table, toss the junk mail, put bills into their respective bin, and place mail specific to each person in the second and third bins.

On Sunday afternoon, when they're getting ready for the week ahead, they each take stuff out of their individual mail bin to sort. Gardiner usually takes his downstairs to his office; Sarah puts hers in her briefcase to take to work. The whole process takes about two minutes, and doesn't require much thought because now it has become an established routine. As an added bonus, they feel as if they're starting the week with a clean slate—not faced with mountains of paper.

Once a week they clean out the bins. The net result is a kitchen that is presentable to the outside world and makes them feel like they're staying on top of the clutter.

Out-of-control clutter can really add up. In an article by Christopher Anderson in the *San Antonio Express-News*, Richard Goldsmith actually kept his catalogs for a year. Thirty-seven companies sent more than 1,800 catalogs to his home in a single year and they weighed in at 494 pounds. Your pile could end up larger; Richard recalled requesting only one catalog, ever.

Find Your Vulnerability and Create Your Personalized Game Plan for Change

Some of you have easily identified in your head one room you need to tackle first. For others, like Alicia, choosing just one room seems like a difficult chore at best.

"There are several places in my house that attract clutter and chaos. My husband's home office always looks like a tornado smashed through it. Okay, it's a small tornado, I admit, but his room's door is the first I close when company comes over. Our kitchen is also a trouble spot like it is for Sarah, except that our kitchen counter, not the table, is the space where our fertile mail piles grow larger each day. Our family room is filled with Lucy's pink plastic Polly Pockets and blond Barbies lounging on the sofas. I still always need to remind myself to just pick one mess at a time to address."

If you are having trouble deciding which one room you should pick to tackle, here are a couple of quick exercises that just might be of help. The first is called Realtor Role-play. Close your eyes and imagine that you have just decided to put your house on the market and you have called over your town's top Realtor to take on the listing. He or she has come over, taken a brief look around, snooped in all of your closets, and now recommends you address several items before the *For Sale* sign goes up on the front lawn. What is the one room or area in the house the Realtor would recommend you clean up? What would he or she say you need to do to that space to get it in order?

Many people find that after just ten minutes of doing this exercise, they have found the area that needs their attention. Still stuck? Did you find that the only decision you've made is to live in your house forever? Have your spouse or a best girlfriend who has spent time at your house try this exercise as well and see what their conclusions are. Someone from the outside will see your home differently than you do.

A second exercise to try is to take a deep, calming breath, then walk into each of your messy rooms and ask yourself two simple questions: how do I feel when I am in this room now? And, how would I feel if this room was clean and orderly? Understanding which room causes you the most anxiety and which one will give you the greatest sense of peace of mind when organized should help you to prioritize your options.

Now that you have identified that *one* room in your house that is your worst organizational issue, you need to take the first steps to get the matter under control. For most people, the problem room is either the home office/family workspace, the kitchen, or the family room. In this next section, we are going to take each one of these rooms and give you a road map to get the chaos under control.

Before we do that, you need to first answer one important question: what is the one main purpose of the room you are going to get Buttoned Up? Sounds simple, but in order to be successful in what you're about to do, you need to first know what you are really trying to achieve. Take the family room. For Holly, a mother of three elementary school–aged kids who are six, seven, and nine, the family room is not just a place to watch TV, play video games, and hang out. The room is also where the kids' computer is set up and where they do their homework. To both get the clutter under control and address the dual needs of the space, Holly divided the room with open bookcases so that one area was for fun and one was for getting stuff done. It made the room more useful and was easier to keep under control.

The Home Office

If your home office is your biggest organizational challenge, you are not alone. Almost 80 percent of today's information is still paper based,[2] and it is commonly estimated that forty-five new sheets of paper are generated each day for each office. The most common offenders in home offices are the overflowing mail and bill piles and the lack of a simple system to file important items away. Start by setting aside four half-hour block increments in one week, to initially get this room under control. Try to make one substantial change in each uninterrupted half-hour block of time.

Step 1: Trash, Return, and Store

Get three large garbage bags or boxes and label them *trash*, *someplace else*, and *stays*. Go through your home office item by item and place everything that is in view (e.g., on the desk, on shelves, counters, on the floor) in one of the three boxes.

Supplies to Button Up
the Home Office

- Three large garbage bags or boxes, labeled *trash*, *someplace else*, and *stays*
- Storage and organizational tools: shelves, bookcases, dry erase board, in-box/out-box, letter sorter, bill holder
- Elegant board box to store papers
- Trash can(s)

After the items in view are tackled, you can then go through any closets, boxes, cabinets, or drawers in the office if you feel they need attention, too.

- *Trash,* rather obviously, are all the things you've been meaning to toss out but haven't; anything with outdated information, etc.

- *Someplace else* are all the items that migrate from other rooms where they really belong: toys, books, clothing, etc. They can also be things that you no longer need and want to sell or give away.

- *Stays* are all the items that you designate as belonging in the office and that contribute to the work you get done there. This includes, but is not limited to, stationery, pens, pencils, Post-its, etc.

When you have done this, throw out the *trash* box. Remove the *someplace else* box from the room. It now has things in it that go elsewhere in the house, or that you want to sell or donate. Come back to these items after you complete the next step and bring them to their proper homes.

Step 2: Design the Stage

Now that you have the items that will remain in your office in one pile, you need to establish the right framework to keep all of that stuff in order. Think about the space vertically as well as horizontally. Can you put in tall shelves or bookcases to house all of the items? Can you store items in bins under a sofa or desk? A bulletin board or dry erase board works well for notices and reminders. Other useful items to use in your home office are an in-box and out-box, letter sorter, and bill holder. Get an elegant printed board box and use it to store papers or items that you don't currently use but may want to use in the future. Put items you rarely need access to—like your children's artwork you are saving—up high and bills and checkbooks that you use often at eye level or below. The more storage space you can create, the more you can find a home for everything. Do not forget to also have one or two trash cans (one for garbage, one for recycling) on hand to make it easy to throw out unnecessary objects immediately. (Buttons 5 and 7, pages 77 and 125, will also help you devise simple systems to file and maintain this central information area for the family.)

Step 3: Ten Minutes a Week

Once the home office is under control, set aside ten minutes each week to throw out the unnecessary items and to remove items that do not belong there (your kids' markers and the cosmetics you bought on your last Target outing) so that all you have left to worry about are the things that need to have a home in the home office. Unless you're superwoman with the pen and the checkbook, after you've used these ten minutes to make sure your office papers and supplies are all in their correct homes, you'll probably need to set aside some additional time for paying your bills, catching up on your e-mail, filing, etc.

Make those ten minutes part of your Sunday afternoon or night—getting ready for the coming week. Once you get the ten-minute habit in place, you will be better able to stay on top of your tasks. Sarah calls that time "recompression"—the bookend to her "decompression" TGIF time on Friday evening.

If Sunday doesn't work for you, choose your own time. A regular day and time earmarked for your weekly straightening will help make this step attainable and maintainable.

The Kitchen

Whoever said the kitchen was just for cooking and eating certainly never came to our houses for dinner. For us (and probably many of you) the kitchen is also a dumping ground for mail, school papers, spare change, jackets, keys, cell phones, and backpacks. There is also the common issue of how to organize the kitchen and pantry so that it works for your family. Where does everything go? How do you make it easy for everyone to pitch in and keep the kitchen neat and the pantry and refrigerator stocked? Try taking one hour a day, for two days, to get your kitchen in order.

Step 1: Tame the Outsiders

The first step to getting the kitchen in order is to make a quick list of all of the clutter items that seem to collect in this room. These kitchen invaders can include spare change, mail, cell phones, keys, purses, backpacks, and lots and lots of mail and newspapers. What is it for you? While you might think the

Supplies to Button Up the Kitchen

- Pencil and pen to make a list of clutter culprits
- Labeled containers, one for each member of the family
- Bowl or hook for keys
- Risers for kitchen cabinets
- Magnetic pad for shopping list

answer is to banish these items from the kitchen, trust us, that probably will not happen. Ingrained habits are hard to break so it's not worth wasting the energy trying. Instead, determine places to keep the mess contained. That old saying of "a place for everything and everything in its place" is one to live by here. First, define what area in your kitchen will house this stuff. Maybe it is part of the kitchen counter, or the end of the kitchen table or even a shelf or two you can hang on the wall. Once you have that area defined, purchase some simple containers and label them accordingly. You can make designated hooks for backpacks or purses, boxes for winter items, a bowl or hook for keys. Each family member can have his or her own designated in-box or bin for their keys, mail, cell phone, etc. That way, they are contained *and* there will be less time spent searching for missing items.

Step 2: Organize the Food

We often hear comments from people who complain that they can never seem to get their pantry together. There are a few simple things you can do to set up the pantry to solve this common problem. First, make sure that you can see everything you have in the pantry. If you do not have a lot of shelves, consider buying risers that allow you to see each can and bottle by putting each item on a different level. Then embrace the FIFO method (accounting and computing speak for first in, first out) and when you replenish items, put them behind the older items. That way you won't get stuck with food past its expiration date. Over-the-door shelving or shelving you can anchor to the back of the door, is an easy way to add storage on your pantry for smaller items like spices and seasonings, Jell-O and pudding boxes, etc. Finally, organize your shelves and the refrigerator so that every member can have easy access to the food they want to eat. Put food for the children on lower shelves. House those pricey gourmet goodies and grown-up drinks on higher shelves.

Step 3: Make Replenishment Easy

A large part of keeping a kitchen together is to make sure it is always stocked with the food that everyone wants to eat along with the basic staples of bread, milk, juice. Often grocery shopping becomes just the mom's responsibility. In the spirit of delegating to other members of the family, create an easy way to get every family member to tell you what they want or need. Put a magnetic pad for shopping lists, as well as a weekly list of usual items, on the refrigerator with a pen tied to it. Ask everyone to write down items that they use up or things that they want to have in the house. Once you institute the "only what is on the list gets in the shopping cart" policy, you will easily get everyone to pitch in and add to the shopping list. But notify your children that Mom's veto power can be used on a list consisting of just junk food—candy, chips, and soda. Consider using an online shopping site that saves a weekly repeating grocery list and delivers them to your home. You can receive your weekly, usual groceries without even leaving the house!

The Family Room/Living Room

Before beginning your cleanup and organizing, think for a minute or two about how the room is used. Do your kids use this room to do homework? Is it the entertainment hub of the house with DVD player, games, and big-screen TV? Is it where you often eat meals and snacks because that kitchen table has piles of mail and newspapers on it? Once you have determined what you want the room to be used for, taking care of a few of the usual suspects should help you keep this area under control. Give yourself four thirty-minute time slots to tame this beast.

Step 1: House the Sprawl

Following the previous guidelines for the home office, get everything that doesn't belong in the room out with a some-place else bag or box. Are your remotes always in a remote location? Repeat after us . . . everything needs a home. For starters, locate or purchase a box or bin to contain all of the remotes. Then put a white Avery label on the back of each stating what the remote is for and in very simple terms, how to use it. Having them labeled means no one is left yelling for audio-visual help. DVDs, CDs, and video games are another issue. If you do not want to take the time and expense to store the DVDs and CDs digitally, then get inexpensive disk holders that are like photo albums with big plastic sectioned pages. Put the DVDs and CDs all in there and throw out all of the empty boxes and cases. Toys also need their own home.

Supplies to Button Up Your Family Room/Living Room

- Box or bin for remotes
- White Avery-brand labels
- Wooden toy chest or colorful toy bins
- Bin or basket for magazines and newspapers
- Two or more trash cans
- Tray to collect dishes

A great solution is a wooden toy chest. But if that is too expensive, there are lots of colorful bins out there for less than $20 that easily store things like board games, dolls, cars, keyboards, or puzzles. It will make a huge difference to have the toys more consolidated and stored compactly. Finally, have a newspaper and magazine bin for all of the family room reading material. You can sort out the old newspapers weekly and the old magazines monthly. When the new issue of a magazine comes in, the old issue should go out.

Step 2: Clean the Mess

Any room in the house can get messy but a room that most of the family uses on a regular basis is sure to be a difficult one to keep neat and tidy. First, get at least two trash cans and place them in the room where people are most apt to want to just leave something rather than walk over and throw it away. Having two may seem like overkill, but trust us, it's essential for a trash can to be reachable in as few steps as possible. Otherwise, those magazines may disintegrate on the coffee table. A good place for them is usually on either side of a couch or by the couch and a lounge chair. Closed swinging-lid trash cans are a good choice if you're concerned about aesthetics. Whatever style trash can you select, the proximity of the trash can will make it easy for everyone to pitch in and clean up.

If your family eats in the family room, dirty dishes can be a problem. It would be nice to get everyone to make sure their dishes are taken to the kitchen and put in the sink but if that's a challenge to delegate, here is one possible work-around. Alicia's sister found a solution for when their children and grandchildren visit. She puts out a tray and asks everyone to put their mess on the tray. Once a day the tray can be picked up and taken to the kitchen.

Step 3: "Commercially" Clean

Once a week when the family is all together watching TV, take the time during commercial breaks to tidy up the room. This would be a great time to encourage your children to put away their toys, books, puzzles, or dress-up clothes in the closet or bins/toy chest you purchased earlier. If you've got more than one problem area in the room, have the entire family focus one full commercial break on each area. You will be amazed what a few people can accomplish in just two minutes and two seconds! In the course of an hour of *Grey's Anatomy*, the family room will be all together and Buttoned Up.

The Big Payoff

The payoff from dealing with one room can be fantastic! Pay attention to changes in your levels of stress. If you find another room or area in the house that has started to cause you anxiety, use the same process to Button Up that other trouble spot. Do you feel relaxed in a way that seems familiar? If you notice how much better you feel, you're not the only one. Forty-eight percent of the women surveyed by Buttoned Up said that they believe that cleaning out their closets can be more gratifying than sex![4]

Button 4: Pick a Room and Get Started

Take a mental walk around your home to pinpoint your trouble spots. "Feel" your way there by noticing which room or part of a room makes you tense. Three points to remember as you work on this room:

1. **It doesn't have to be perfect.** Chasing the unattainable, like a flawless kitchen table, can get you stuck and prevent you from making a change.

2. **Focus on what's important.** Changes that would most impact the way the room looks, work. What consequences (such as an unpaid bill or a missed social opportunity) can result from not making a change?

3. **Ask for help.**

The Home Office

1. Divide stuff into boxes labeled *trash, someplace else,* and *stays.*

2. Establish a framework to keep all the stuff in order; everything needs a home.

3. Take ten minutes a week to throw out and sort.

The Kitchen

1. Take inventory—determine what is actually in your kitchen and make a home for it.

2. Organize shelves and the refrigerator so everyone can see the food they eat and the oldest food is in the front.

3. Keep a list on the refrigerator with the policy "if it's not on the list, it won't get in the shopping cart."

The Family Room/Living Room

1. Get a box for the remotes, disk holders for DVDs or CDs, boxes for children's toys, and magazine bins for periodicals.

2. Keep trash cans in the room and use a tray for dishes or institute a paper-only rule.

3. Get the whole family to help "commercially" clean during TV commercials.

Set Up a Control Center

Welcome to the age of overload. Today we have more of everything: news and information, e-mail, regular mail, voice mail, appointments, things to buy, and ways to pay. When you multiply the impact of this overload by the number of people in your household, it can get downright overwhelming. Our home is the center of a circulatory system that keeps our families together and moving forward. The problem is overloaded systems don't function well. The more things you have to navigate around, consider, respond to, or accomplish in a typical day, the harder it is to maintain any semblance of control.

If you've ever felt the stress of having to deal with two weeks' worth of mail, thousands of e-mails, and five loads of laundry after coming back from vacation, you know what a clogged system feels like. The last thing you want is to feel that way on a daily basis.

Sometimes, however, we neglect to do the simple things that are necessary for keeping our figurative pathways clean, open, and healthy. We too often find out the cost of a clogged system can be high. For example, the difference between landing a new job or remaining unemployed might hinge on reading an e-mail alerting you to a job interview, getting the appointment time onto a central family calendar, and coordinating your family's schedule around that appointment so you are free to go.

The benefits from a highly functioning system are high. Plans are made, appointments are kept, your family's home, work, school, social, and athletic activities operate without a hitch. And, if there is a hitch, then you have the ability to cope. The key is to make some changes in how you've been running things and try some new approaches on for size.

Everyone organizes their home systems in a slightly different way—your own "home healthy" system will be different from your best friend's. In this chapter, as throughout the book, we encourage you to put your own unique style into the Control Center system you adopt. Make sure it's attractive to you and works for you and your family. Test it out, try variations, talk about it with your family. Remember that effective change can take willpower and time.

Once you understand the major flows of information and stuff into and out of your home, the trick to staying on top of it is to set up a Control Center. Think of it as a central clearinghouse of sorts that is equipped with some effective filters for organizing, categorizing, and otherwise handling it all. The solution is a Control Center in your home that will be an area where dates, schedules, notes, and messages that impact the individuals in a family as well as the family as a whole can be handled efficiently.

When your home works more efficiently, you'll notice the difference. You'll have more productive family members, more hugging and smiling, and less yelling. You'll find your peaceful, healthy home is beautiful in a way that is deep, satisfying, and personal.

The Organizational Components of Your Home

So what are the areas of a home that are most prone to overload, blockages, and backups? We've found that every home has the same four areas that are the repositories for information, keep the house running, or maintain order.

#1: The in-box. The in-box is responsible for all of the communications to, from, and with every member of your family. It encompasses voice mail, e-mail, snail mail, BlackBerry messages, text messages, instant messages, and pages. In a world where the methods of communication are ever expanding, it's easy to see how this channel could become overloaded. Of course, some in-box items go out through the mail, e-mail, the trash, or other means, but for simplicity here we'll simply refer to this area as the in-box.

#2: The schedule. The schedule, formalized or not, juggles and aligns the multitude of demands on everybody's time. It includes everyday obligations, appointments, extracurricular activities, and special events for everybody in the household. It's easy to see how the pressure we're all under to cram as much as we can into a finite number of hours could cause serious stress here.

#3: The chores. Chores promote the basic functionality and cleanliness of the home. This covers the duties of taking out the garbage, doing the housecleaning, the dishes, the laundry, and caring for the yard. If chores aren't evenly distributed or there isn't enough time in the week to do them, the physical clutter and mess will undoubtedly accumulate, damming up the works.

#4: The stuff. The physical goods for each person in a household must actually fit in the house. This pertains to all the trappings of life: personal belongings such as toys, clothes, and knickknacks. Think about moving every item in your house and then you realize how much stuff is in your home. In a country where the average person spends between 88 and 96 percent of their disposable income on items for personal consumption,[1] it's easy to see how this area can become seriously clogged. Thank goodness the cure for overload in this area is so straightforward: the trash can and its two cousins, namely the recycle bin and the box earmarked for the secondhand shop.

All the areas interconnect. Mail can get lost in a room cluttered with too much stuff. E-mails often contain information that needs to get added into the family schedule. Chores keep the physical aspects of your home clean, orderly, and accessible. These four basic concepts are simply a flexible framework to start you thinking about the flow of your home, see where you can unclog problem areas, and institute new methods for keeping the information flowing so your family won't get lost in clutter and confusion.

Common Trouble Spots

If your home has backups in one of these areas, something isn't right, and you know it. What exactly is clogged? Having gone through the first few buttons and targeted a problem room in your home, take some time to think about where information isn't flowing, where you hit snags in getting things done, or keeping a clean space. In the following pages you will find some examples and some symptoms of clogs that may help diagnose your own home situation. Remember that your goal is not to be perfect or to be like your friend. Your goal is to make your own life as efficient, productive, and rewarding as you can, and to reduce your own stress.

Most people have fairly easily identifiable problem spots. For Kieran, it's the in-box and the schedule. "Between snail mail, e-mail, voice mail, and text messages, I have to process well over one hundred and fifty pieces of communication a day. It's a constant source of disorganization for me—physically and mentally. My other trouble spot is the schedule. As a magazine editor, work life is hectic and there are often long hours right before an issue closes. I'm also stepping into the role of stepparent to two beautiful and rambunctious boys, which is great, but requires a whole new level of discipline around scheduling. I simply can't afford to be disorganized when it comes to our new family schedule. I have to make sure that I'm coordinating with my fiancé at all times to ensure that we're where the boys need us to be when they need us to be there."

Family members often have different "pinch points" or trouble areas. For Jenny the trouble spot is also the in-box. "I'm often stressed with the overwhelming amount of messages I have to sort through. It's mind-boggling how many messages from all different sources I have to respond to every day. And I feel compelled to answer every one within twenty-four hours, which, when you consider the volume, can seriously impact my ability to get anything else done. My husband, Dave, has a different challenge. His trouble spot is stuff. More specifically, he has a penchant for electronic gadgets and fun toys for our daughter.

That means our living space (and cars) are often overflowing with these electronic items."

For many women, particularly those juggling careers and families, chores represent a real problem area. For Marci, a freelance lawyer and mother of four, chores are a constant source of clogs. "My husband runs a small business and is often traveling, so the responsibility for most household chores, from picking up dry cleaning to making dinner and taking out the trash, falls on my shoulders. My youngest, age two, is really too little to do more than help pick up his toys and put them away. And as the family's de facto cabdriver, I spend so much time shuttling little people to and from soccer games, swim practice, ballet lessons, Spanish lessons, etc., that I often fall behind on the chore front. If I get the recycling bins out to the curb in time every other week, I'm doing well! But I have to admit, falling behind on even those little things makes me feel out of control and cranky."

Symptoms That Might Indicate a Clog

- You've noticed your kids going through the dirty clothes hamper to find something to wear to school.

- There are friends whom you avoid saying hello to on the street because you're so embarrassed that you never responded to a written party invitation that they sent you.

- Trash cans never get emptied without yelling or whining.

- You can't park your car in your garage because it's filled with boxes from your last move that you haven't sorted through yet.

- There are undated items in your fridge that you're afraid to eat, like those cocktail onions you bought for your father-in-law when he visited eight months ago, but because they *might* be good, you don't want to throw them out, either.

- Your child's coach won't let her play in the soccer games because you keep forgetting to take her to practice.

- Your bedroom is a stubbed toe waiting to happen because there are so many clothes, books, and bags on the floor.

- Your dishes seem to live in the sink instead of the cupboard.

- You're concerned about your credit rating because you've lost some bills.

- You seem to be buying more and more belated birthday cards.

- You have a lot of "twins" in your stuff because you've bought a second copy of a book or CD when you can't find the one you already have.

- Because your list of unread e-mail is too long you realize you're missing meetings, deadlines, and other essential information.

If any items from this list resonate with you, join the club! Sounds like (A) you have a normal family that isn't perfect and (B) you're one step closer to understanding which clogs your Control Center can help to loosen.

Setting Up a Control Center

If the thought of setting up a Control Center seems daunting, rest assured it doesn't need to be complicated at all. Again, you are creating a Control Center to help with your particular needs. It's a personalized system but all Control Centers will have some features in common. The Control Center must be in a central location so that it is easy for all family members to access and use. Ideally, put it close to where you usually drop the mail, since one of its main functions is to keep what comes in the post under control.

The Control Center has some basic ingredients for processing and recording information. You may choose only some of these ingredients, or you may think of others. The recipe for creating your own Control Center is very personal and customizable.

- Trash can

- Large flat surface for sorting papers and envelopes near where you drop the mail

- Letter holder or letter tray with approximately five slots or compartments for sorting the incoming and outgoing mail

- Large month-at-a-glance calendar, either paper or a whiteboard, with squares for each day that are large enough to write in

- A place to post everyone's weekly schedule and chores; each family member gets one line for their schedule, and the columns are the days of the week

- A place, a whiteboard or bulletin board, to write notes and leave them where others can see them

- Post-its to leave notes on the incoming mail

- Pens or pencils

There is not one cookie-cutter solution or one-size-fits-all answer to building your own family Control Center. We have found that in order to set up a successful Control Center, it must fit into the way you currently live your life and not require you to dramatically change your already established habits and routines.

There are a few questions we find are helpful to ask yourself to determine how to best set up your own system.

1. **How can I make this system easy to set up?** How much time am I *happy* to commit to getting this done? For example, Susan gave herself three hours and included a trip to Target to buy supplies. Beth, on the other hand, was only happy to commit an hour to this project.

2. **What will make a Control Center simple for me and my family to use and to maintain?** It may be that each person needs to be responsible for their own daily activities and mail. Maybe you need to sort through the mail only once a week. Remember, the only right answers are the ones that work for you.

3. **Where is the best place to locate my Control Center?** For many people the kitchen is the "heart" of the house and all paths lead to it. Susan has her in-box and calendar in the front hall so you cannot miss it when you come and go. Marci keeps hers in the mudroom just by the garage. You want to choose a location that does not make anyone work to find mail or calendars. Your family should pass by the Control Center several times a day. You also want the

information on the calendar and/or whiteboard or bulletin board to be easy to read for everyone. If you have to decipher scribbles, it won't work.

Techniques for Handling Mail

Let's start by creating the in-box for the family. While this will be primarily mail, it is also important to make space here for phone messages and other communications. The tools are pretty simple: a large trash can, recycle bin, some type of a sorter container, in-box, or mail sorter with around five slots, and a stack of Post-it notes and pens. The Post-its and pens are to jot down notes for follow-ups for family members, and save you time having to search for little scraps of paper to write messages on.

The trash can goes right next to the in-box. If you touch a piece of mail that you know is junk, throw it out immediately. Do not wait. Do not pass GO. Just put it in the trash or recycling bin and forget it.

Once you've got the junk mail out of the way, we suggest you sort mail in up to seven categories. These categories are filters that correspond to the most important areas of your life. You may be able to get away with as few as three; we recommend separating mail into bills, correspondence, and items requiring follow-ups. The simpler the system, the easier it is to use—so avoid the temptation to have a "perfect" filtering system that has a slot for every conceivable piece of information. Because many people have both physical as well as virtual in-boxes, you may want to replicate the same filters in your e-mail system, Black-Berry, or other electronic device. For most people, it does not make sense to sort mail by each member of the household, but if that seems like it might naturally work for you, give it a try.

While all families are different, there are a handful of very common categories that should work for most people. We've listed a few of the most common below. Try to limit yourself to the seven categories that will help you tame the in-box without overthinking it:

- **Bills**

- **Correspondence**—This may include financial and social correspondence.

- **Magazines and catalogs**—Probably a bigger bin than the rest of the sections but not too big, so you are forced to sort through at least once a week.

- **Follow-ups**—Use Post-its to note items requiring follow-ups by one or more members of the family.

- **Notes**—Notes might go in one of the in-boxes or get posted on a bulletin board or a whiteboard; use the boards to leave notes, phone messages, or reminders for the family.

- **School**

- **Work**

Once you select your categories, find the right mail sorter to use. They come in all colors, styles, and prices. Buy what suits your needs. The Container Store and Target are great places to search for options. Do not forget to label your in-box according to which section will be for which type of information.

Now that your in-box is set up, make sure you put it where everyone has easy access and passes by frequently. To maintain your in-box, get into a daily and weekly routine.

Daily: Whoever brings the mail in on any given day can place it by the in-box and sort it by category. This can be done each day and should take no more that two or three minutes. Throw junk mail out first and then simply sort the rest.

Weekly: Once a week go through and do a primary in-box sort to throw out additional items and distribute the follow-up items like bills and correspondence to the appropriate parties. When it comes to paying the bills, you can't afford to be late. We encourage you and anyone else responsible for the household finances to take the three to five minutes to prepare and pay all bills in the in-box once a week. Set a recurring appointment in the books and stick to it. If you decide to hold on to your payment for a few additional days, put it back in the slot for items that need action so you'll know exactly where to find it when you're ready to send it. If you have left your checkbook at work or if you pay your bills online and your Internet connection isn't working, then schedule a window of time the following day to complete the task.

Once you've taken care of the bills, it is the perfect time to recycle magazines that are past their issue date. Alert everyone when you set up the Control Center that if there is something sacred and specific to them in the in-box they should remove it before the weekly dump-and-sort. No matter how you do it, it should be easy and fast and fit into your routine. If it is easy, it will significantly increase the likelihood of you and your family sticking with the mail-sort system three months from now.

I Need to Be Where, When?

The next essential component of the Control Center covers arteries for the schedule and the chores. With agendas overflowing the way they are today in most families, it's essential that you keep track of everybody's schedule in one master location.

There are two rules (although we hate rules, in this case they seem to work) to follow that will make a family calendar and schedule work:

1. **A family calendar and schedule must be easily shared.** That means it is most likely paper based, not electronic, and needs to be out where everyone can see it, change it, and add to it.

2. **Each person in the family over the age of ten should be responsible each week for filling in their own information.** If you think it will be hard to get your child to do this, follow the rule "if it isn't written down, it doesn't get done." The first time Logan didn't write down his baseball practice and Marci refused to take him was enough incentive for him to do a perfect job with his schedule.

We find that it's most effective to post both a weekly routine and a monthly calendar to mark variances from the weekly routine. One easy way to keep track of both is to post two dry erase boards next to each other in the kitchen, on the back of the pantry door, or other common area. One dry erase board should be a large (24"×36"), preformatted calendar with a month at a glance, and the other should be a similarly sized dry erase board that also has a bulletin surface.

Use the plain whiteboard to keep track of everybody's regular weekly schedule. Assuming weekly schedules don't vary from week to week, if you write down each person's regularly scheduled activities once on the "master schedule" board you save yourself the time of having to rewrite the same thing week after week in a planner. Give each person in the family a row and mark each day of the week across the top of each of seven columns. Then write down each person's regular weekly schedule, or if everyone is over the age of ten, they should fill in their schedule. It's easier to distinguish family members if each person has their own color—but it is not necessary. Keep paper schedules from classes and extracurricular activities posted on the bulletin portion of the board so you can see when the schedule will change. Typical items in the weekly routine include:

- Sports practices and games (if at regular set times and days)

- School

- Work

- Lessons (e.g., piano, golf, etc.)

- Day care

- Chores

- Regular appointments

- A regularly scheduled family night

Use the month-at-a-glance calendar to mark special events or deviations from the master schedule. This is where you put all of the information that varies from the weekly routine, from birthday parties and dinners to other events. Again, this should be listed by person, and if you're color-coding, be sure to use the same ink color per person that is used in the schedule. Examples of what may typically go onto the monthly calendar include:

- Travel schedules

- Specific notes about sports events (e.g., what field, what jersey to wear)

- Car pools

- Recitals

- Babysitters

- Family vacations

We find that the combination of these two tools makes for a family calendar that is relatively easy to maintain and yet fairly detailed on where everyone needs to be and when.

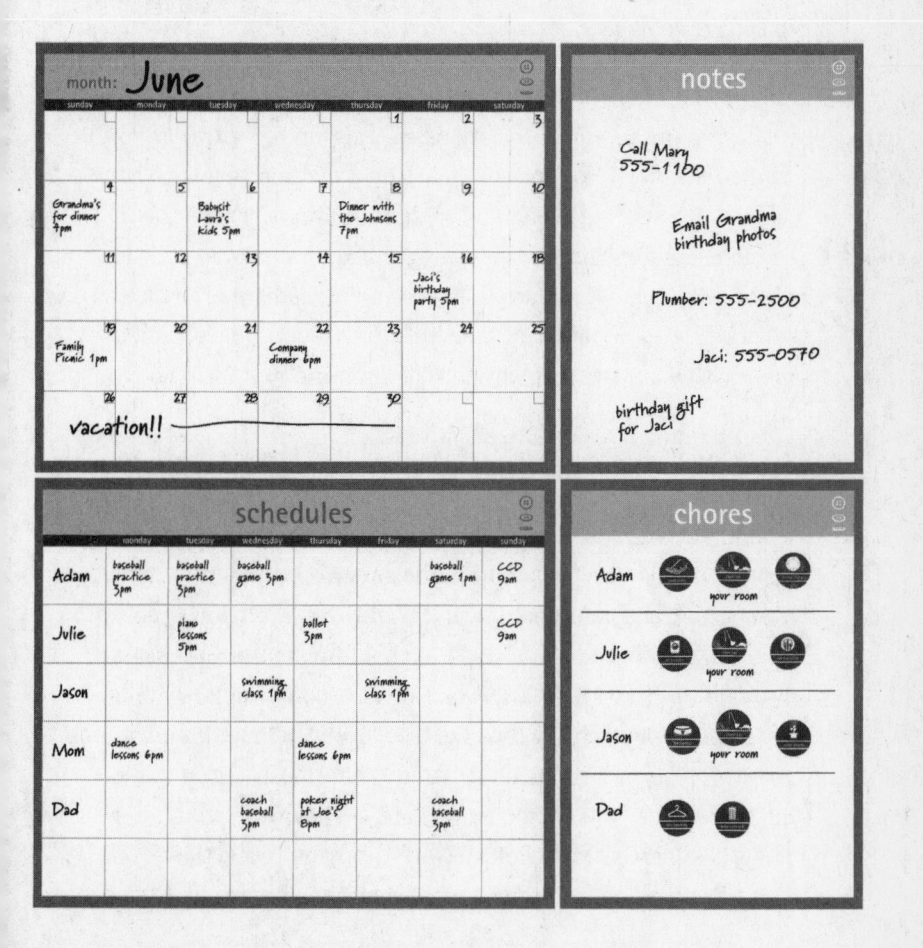

If you're pressed for space, use a simple 8½" × 11" sheet for the calendar and another for the schedule. Ideally, they should still be placed in a spot that is easy for all family members to interact with, like taped to the refrigerator, for example. If you don't have room to post them there, make sure each family member over the age of ten has a chance to input their information and verify that it is correct.

How the Control Center Worked for Kieran and Marci in Different Ways

For both Kieran and Jenny, who have issues managing the sheer volume of communications, setting up a central in-box worked wonders. For both of them, the issue was volume. They needed a system that enabled them to dump or ignore the incoming communications that were junk and filter what was left so they could identify ones that were an immediate priority. To solve her mail problem, Kieran set up three in-boxes in both the physical and virtual worlds. The first one was for financial communications related to the household, such as bills, tax items, and invoices from the contractor. This is always the "high priority" file. The second was for communications related to family schedules, like music class and doctors' appointments for the family. The last was for social correspondence—notes from friends, restaurant openings, and the like. Now, everything that comes into the house (or her e-mail in-box) must go into one of those three buckets. She also bought a fancy, new trash can to put right by the mail drop. Now, her fiancé and she take turns sorting the mail. Anything that doesn't fit in one of the three buckets is tossed immediately. They were a little nervous that such a draconian rule—to throw out everything that didn't fit—would mean they'd toss something important. But so far, all they've thrown out is junk. For those virtual items that arrive to each of them that they both need to review, they made a pact to summarize in one e-mail that they send to the other person once a day.

They were also bad at remembering to check the answering machine at home, so they were always missing opportunities to get together with friends and family. Since they never checked that "in-box," they figured out a way to send the information collected from that particular in-box to in-boxes they did check—namely, their e-mail in-boxes. They signed up for a voice over Internet protocol (VoIP) service, that delivers the phone service through cable or DSL lines and now both receive voice mail messages from their home phone into their e-mail in-boxes—simultaneously!

For Marci, having a central clearinghouse for the family calendar turned out to be a godsend. "My husband and I each tended to keep our schedules on our individual computers, which had no way of syncing to a master family calendar. When one of us wanted to schedule something, we never knew the impact on the other person until a conflict hit us in the face at the eleventh hour. To complicate matters, my three school-age kids (Logan, Harry, and Megan) were constantly bringing home random slips of paper with important scheduling information, and I lived in mortal fear of losing or misplacing that information."

Marci tried every online calendar imaginable and none worked. "None were compatible with a Mac (me and my children) and a PC (my husband). The other drawback was that they weren't visible to everybody. Ultimately we created a family calendar that has three parts: The first is our weekly schedules—where I can also see where others can help me with those household chores. The second is a month-at-a-glance calendar to note deviations from the norm and the third is a Post-it notepad so we can alert each other to apparent conflicts, where we have flexibility, and so on. We put it in a central place so that everybody can interact with it, not just me."

Chores

While everyone in your family is in a learning mode and adjusting to the Control Center, you have a perfect opportunity to adjust chore responsibilities in your home.

Assigning chores is a great way to share the load and keep your home cleaner, less cluttered, and a more comfortable and stress-free place to live. Although you may not hear a thank-you from a child who is assigned to help with laundry, trash, dishes, or cooking, just wait a while. We've talked with many young adults who were glad they learned housekeeping skills before they urgently needed them at college or when they started living on their own.

When you start assigning some family chores, consider these ideas:

Start small, go slowly, go long: Suzanne has started her five-year-old daughter on making her own bed and clearing her plate from the table. "She likes taking her plate away, and her bed is lumpy, but it's made!" says Suzanne. Add more responsibilities gradually. Just like our bodies grow slowly from when we are children to adults—a few inches of height a year—chore responsibilities can grow slowly over a long period of time.

Do the chores with them: Most people like help when they're learning something new, and jobs are more fun when they are shared. For a while, you may feel like the reduction in your workload isn't obvious, but eventually others will take on their chores and you can let go of physical support and simply become the cheerleader. Review Button 3: You Don't Need to Do Everything Yourself, for tips on delegating effectively.

Aim for equality: Chores are a sign of adulthood, and everyone—no matter what their age or gender—can contribute to the home with their efforts on a regular basis. A great way to check up on if the chores are being done is to create a simple chore chart and have your kids chart their own successes with gold star stickers.

With more regular, small amounts of time spent on keeping your home organized, you will begin to see the difference. You might even stop dreaming about moving into a larger home for all of your stuff. The National Association of Professional Organizers says that 80 percent of the clutter in your home is a result of disorganization, not a lack of space![2]

Reinforcing Using the Control Center

Even the most attractive Control Center isn't artwork to be admired. Instead, its motto should be "please touch." How can you help your Control Center get integrated into your home? Unlike a new baby or puppy, it won't speak for itself by being cute and cuddly and loud. For a while, you'll need to be your Control Center's ally, cheerleader, and enforcer. Here are some ideas that may help.

Enforce deadlines: Marjorie Blanchard once said, "A goal is just a dream with a deadline." Set deadlines for putting

List of Common Family Chores

Inside Chores

Clean your room, age 4 and up

Collect the trash, age 6 and up

Clean the bathroom, age 10 and up

Vacuum and sweep, age 8 and up

Do laundry, age 10 and up

Wash the windows, age 10 and up

Water the plants, age 7 and up

Clean the fish tank, age 13 and up

Empty the cat litter, age 7 and up

Outside Chores

Put out the trash, age 7 and up

Cut the grass, age 13 and up

Wash the car, age 10 and up

Clean out the car, age 7 and up

information into and taking information out of the Control Center, and stick to them. For example, you might choose to go through your mail every Sunday or say that any carpooling request that isn't on the calendar by then will simply not happen.

Reward, reward, reward: Pay attention to when the Control Center system is working well. When it is, crow about it! For

List of Common Family Chores

Everyday Chores

Make your bed, age 5 and up

Brush your teeth, age 2 and up

Floss your teeth, age 5 and up

Set the table, age 5 and up

Clear the table, age 5 and up

Wash the dishes, age 7 and up

Feed the pet, age 7 and up

Walk the dog, age 8 and up

Put away toys, age 4 and up

Empty the dishwasher, age 5 and up

Help with dinner prep, age 8 and up

Take a bath or shower, age 5 and up

humans, as with our beloved pets, prompt and consistent rewards are the secret to changing behavior. Reward yourself and others with kind words or a special treat. We've found that special desserts often work well for reinforcing the use of the Control Center. Also, you'll see that using the Control Center is its own reward because you'll have a system for getting things done on time, and getting the family where they need to be for work, school, or special events.

Talk about things that need improvement: No one was born knowing how to use a Control Center. It's a learning process.

When appointments get missed, or mail gets lost, don't panic. Talk about what happened. Figure out how to handle the same situation better the next time. Learn from it, and move on. One more thing: notice that you're moving, and the clogs are clearing. Congratulations!

Button 5:
Set Up a Control Center

The power of a Control Center is that it is a central clearing-house for your home, equipped with some effective filters for organizing, categorizing, and otherwise handling it all. Make sure it is attractive to you and works for your family.

Visualize the flexible framework of the organizational components of your home and how the information flows. The Control Center can help you see where you can unclog the problem areas, and institute new methods for keeping the information flowing.

Area 1: The in-box—voice mail, e-mail, snail mail

Area 2: The schedule—tells where-and-when routines for school, work, lessons, sports practices, chores, day care, babysitters, leisure

Area 3: The chores—carpooling, laundry, lawn mowing, dishes, cooking, trash collection

Area 4: The stuff—every purchase your family makes that takes up space

Compile the ingredients of a Control Center:

- Trash can and recycle bin

- Desk or counter surface

- In-box

- Large month-at-a-glance calendar

- A place to put weekly schedules and chores

- A place to write and post notes

- Post-its

- Pens/pencils

Possible categories for mail filters:

- **Bills**

- **Correspondence**—This may include financial and social correspondence.

- **Magazines and catalogs**—Probably a bigger bin than the rest of the sections but not too big, so you are forced to sort through at least once a week.

- **Follow-ups**—Items requiring follow-ups by one of more members of the family. You can use Post-its to indicate who needs to do what and at what time.

- **Notes**—A place to leave notes, phone messages, etc., for anyone in the family. This might go in one of the in-boxes or get posted on a bulletin board or a whiteboard.

- **School**

- **Work**

In-box success means a daily and weekly dump-and-sort—sort items by category each day, and toss junk mail. In the weekly dump-and-sort, throw out additional items, sort magazines, and follow up on bills and correspondence, handle individual mail, tell everyone that anything left will be tossed.

A successful family calendar and schedule must be easily shared, and each person over ten should be responsible for filling in their own information. "If it's not written down, it doesn't get done."

To help get the chores done:

- Start small, go slowly, go long

- Do the chores with them

- Aim for equality

- Enforce deadlines

- Reward, reward, reward

- Talk about things that need improvement

Put Technology to Work for You

There's a scene in a movie we love called *Office Space* where the three beleaguered main characters reach their breaking point with a semi-functional fax machine. In a moment of madness, they abscond with it in the trunk of their car, drive to an abandoned lot, and "jump" it in a gang-inspired melee. In slow motion, faces contorted with the rage of the oppressed, they exact their revenge for all of the fax machine's nonsensical error codes, paper jams, and time-wasting bugs. They smash it to smithereens with baseball bats, hard fists, and a series of swift kicks. Only when the annoying contraption has been reduced to a pile of rubble do their faces finally relax; with the machine gone, they're back in control.

If you've ever had such an *Office Space* moment of your own (or wished you could have one) then you know that when technology works for you, your new product becomes your new best friend. But when it doesn't, you hate it because it's invasive and disruptive to your life.

Cell phones are the perfect example of technology at its best. Jenny muses, "Cell phones are miracles. I save so much time because of mine that I would be utterly lost without it. I use it to make calls whenever and wherever, to get directions when I'm lost, to ask my husband to pick the dry cleaning up when I know he's going to be driving past the shop, and on and on. In fact, it's difficult to remember how we ever survived without them. As a sign of how much they are part of our lives, one of my daughter's first toys was a plastic cell phone that she just loved to carry around and talk into, just like Mommy and Daddy."

In other cases, technology isn't always such a miracle. Nancy turned to an electronic device in an attempt to stay ahead of her in-box. "I bought a BlackBerry a few years ago so

Technophobes Take Heart

If you are intimidated by technology, take heart: you don't need digital devices to get effectively Buttoned Up. If you've tried, but you realized you're an "unplugged" type of person, then don't bother trying to put a digital tool kit together (and go ahead and skip to the next chapter). However, as a general rule, there is a way to approach technology so that it doesn't overwhelm you. We recommend some options toward the end of this chapter that are not too difficult to set up and use. If you're feeling game, test one or two of them. You never know, you could be more digitally proficient than you give yourself credit for.

that I could get e-mail anywhere. I thought that if I wasn't tied to my computer I'd be able to deal with the hundreds of e-mails that I get in a day . . . that I could respond to things in those 'lost little moments.' As it turned out, there was no way to filter the messages coming in. Every time that darn little thing vibrated I felt compelled to drop what I was doing and respond. I was buried in e-mails, unable to concentrate on anything, and anxious all the time. So after a few months, I liberated myself by chucking it into the Pacific Ocean. I haven't regretted it once!"

The trick is to get technology to work *for* you as you move to become more organized.

Using Technology to Get the Job Done and Stay Organized

Following are some pros and cons to consider when you are deciding whether to adopt technology to solve a problem. Remember that using technology isn't a necessity, but it can help to streamline some of your time and tasks. You may find that a little technology goes a long way for you or that you work best when using high-tech gear to get your jobs done. As with everything Buttoned Up, finding the tools that suit you and the tasks at hand is the best way to get yourself organized.

Some points to ponder:

The Upside to Technology

It's searchable. When you keep notes, phone numbers, appointments, names, and addresses on the computer, you can find them quickly. For example, a computer calendar can come in handy when you ask yourself, "Do I already have an appointment for my next annual checkup?" or "When was my last one?"

Information can be saved in a small amount of space. The U.S. produces 250 megabytes of data each year for every man, woman, and child on earth.[1] To give you an idea of how much paper that is, the text of this book can be stored in one megabyte of space. Therefore, on average, every person generates the paper equivalent of 250 books each year. However, a typical home computer with a 100-gigabyte hard disk can hold 100,000 megabytes of data, the equivalent of 100,000 books!

It moves when you do. Cell phones keep you in touch outside of your home or office. The Internet is everywhere. When you're "connected," you can be liberated from the need to be physically next to the machine in order to receive a fax, phone message, or e-mail. With WiFi you can plug in at your local coffee shop or just about anyplace.

Someone has already thought through solving the problem for you. Much of technology and computer software is invented to solve a human dilemma, such as: "How can I walk into my empty home filled with the smells of a home-cooked dinner waiting for me?" (the Crock-Pot), "How can I record TV shows and watch them at the same time?" (TiVo), and "How can I perform the same series of calculations over and over?" (Excel)

Time-shifting. E-mail and voice mail can shift *my* convenient time to *your* convenient time. For example, I pick the time to write the e-mail that's perfect for me (at 3:00 A.M. when

I'm awaked by my snoring partner) and you pick the perfect time to read it (at 11:00 P.M. when you've completed your other tasks for the day).

Easier purchases (no errands) and shipping (no wrapping or mailing of gifts or cards). Buying online can be very efficient, especially if you're buying an item that you won't need to return because you know exactly what you want or because it's a gift. Try your grocery shopping online. You can save a weekly list online for your necessities and your groceries will be shipped right to your door. This is a great weekly time-saver for busy moms.

Immediacy of communication and purchases. Immediacy is a great benefit to the sender, because she knows a receiver can read a message seconds after she clicks "send," as opposed to two to seven days for snail mail. Of course, e-mail readers have to be aware of the temptation to continually read e-mail all day when it's "fresh." To avoid this constant checking of your e-mail, pay close attention to the messages you receive that are labeled "alert" or "urgent." You have the option to send e-mails with an alert to inform the receiver that the e-mail is urgent.

Easier sharing of data and information via the Internet. If you want to share something you've written, photographed, videoed, or recorded, you can quickly e-mail the information or put it online. This allows you to share without, for example, the need to carry around a stack of photos. Try a photo sharing Web site, like Kodak Gallery (www.kodakgallery.com), where you can upload pictures to a shared Web site. All your family members can download their pictures onto the Web site after a family vacation, for example. This way, you can pick and choose what pictures you want to download and print out.

The Downside to Technology

The only thing you need to read a piece of paper is your eyes. Therefore, a piece of paper will always be readable, unlike those old floppy disks you have laying around in your basement.

Selecting the right technology requires time up front to make a good choice. If you are responsible for your own technological purchase, you'll want to take the time to research whether your new acquisition will do the job you need and fits your own personal style of working.

Using a new technological product effectively requires both learning and boot-up time. Turning on a computer can take much longer than opening the cover of a book or a journal—minutes too long when all you want to do is jot down a phone number or look up a quote. Learning to use a new technological product sometimes means you're unlearning an old product, moving data over, and relearning new habits.

Dependence on electricity at the location where you're using the product. For technical products to work, they usually need to be tethered to an electricity outlet (hard to find on a plane) or expensive limited-life batteries that need recharging or replacing.

Problems kick in when technology breaks down or gets old. There is always the dreaded moment when something isn't working and you actually have to read the product manual.

Can you fix it yourself? If not, who do you call? When do you replace the item?

Technological products usually have a shorter lifetime than non-technological ones. How long have you had your favorite book or your hammer? How long have you had the cell phone in your purse?

Writing in your own handwriting exudes your own personal style. A personal handwritten note or your own scribbled journal can express the writer more genuinely than typewritten characters can.

Understanding the Most Popular Technology Options

Understanding some of the basic features of the most popular gadgets and software programs is helpful in determining what options are best suited to your needs. For some people, this section may seem basic, but for others, it is a good refresher course in some of the technology options that can make getting and staying organized easier.

Gadgets 101

1. **Cell phone**—Cell phones today are not only phones but often also include a calendar, instant message capabilities, camera, and an address book. Find an affordable cell plan with good coverage where you live and work.

2. **BlackBerry**—BlackBerrys today come in all shapes and sizes and often have all of the features of a cell phone

along with e-mail, a calendar, and an address book. Especially with the smaller versions like the BlackBerry Pearl, this one device is your phone and portable e-mail gadget all in one.

3. **iPhone**—Everyone has heard of the iPhone and many people are buying them. The iPhone is the true all-in-one gadget. It is your phone, e-mail, calendar, address book, Web browser, iPod, and camera all in one device. With a starting price of around $400, it is expensive, but useful.

4. **PalmPilot**—The Palm or PDA (personal digital assistant) is less common today. Think of it as the BlackBerry without the e-mail capability. It is an electronic calendar and address book.

5. **Broadband card**—Broadband cards insert into your laptop and give you a broadband Internet connection anywhere, at any time all for a monthly fee of around $40. Most wireless carriers have broadband card hardware for sale with the accompanying monthly data plans.

Software 101

1. **Outlook**—Outlook is Microsoft's e-mail software and it is standard fare for most businesses. For almost any e-mail address you have, you can set up to work with Outlook. The program also easily syncs with most Palms, BlackBerrys, and even the iPhone. It is also easy to use for all of your e-mail, contact, and calendar needs.

2. **Google**—Everyone knows Google but Google also has some great features that can help you get organized.

Google Calendar is a shared calendar program that can work for family or professional calendar sharing. Google Alerts can be set up to notify you via e-mail any time a particular event or person is in the news.

3. **Quicken**—Quicken is the standard for home finance management software. It is great for keeping track of spending and managing your finances. There is also a Web-based version of the Quicken software that you can "rent" on an annual basis. This Web-based application is accessible from any location, which makes it easier for busy families to have one central financial "hub."

4. **Instant messaging**—Instant messaging from AIM (www .aim.com), Windows Messenger (http://getlive.com/), and Gchat from Google's Gmail (http://mail.google.com/ mail) are simple programs to instantly text people who are online at the same time you are. Have a text conversation with someone without having to e-mail or pick up the phone.

Making a Great Choice and Avoiding "Buyer's Remorse"

Putting time and thought into your purchase can pay off in the long run. Here are some tips on purchasing technological products.

How Technology Is Like Your Mate

In so many ways finding the right technological tool is like finding a great mate. *Don't expect perfection!*

When it comes to technology, it's easy to get caught up in the fevered swirl of never-ending improvements, or to think, "*If only* I had the latest version of this or that program, all would be right." Yes, a technological improvement can make your job of getting organized easier and possibly more pleasant. However, there are two flaws in expecting the next new thing to be the perfect solution. First, many first-generation products have a lot of bugs because they're less tested, so they tend to be less trustworthy than a product that has been on the market for a while. Secondly, if you're putting off an organizational task because you don't have the latest and greatest gadget or program, perhaps you're simply procrastinating. You'll still have to set aside the time to address an organizational problem or job, technology or not.

Know the Objective

Have you ever purchased an innovative little tool or program because it was "neat" or "cool" and then rationalized to yourself how "useful" it would be only to find it sitting, unused, months later?

Before you put any technology to work for you, ask yourself, "What am I trying to accomplish?" When you have a goal in mind, it is much easier to determine what *won't* help, so you're not easily swayed by slick packaging or promises. It will also help you determine what kind of features and benefits *will* help you get the job done.

The more specifically the objective is defined, the easier it will be to find a tool that can actually help. Try to state your goal in terms of the desired results or outcomes. An outcome is a clear description of what you need to accomplish—with or without the tool. For instance: think about the difference between an ambiguous goal ("get my bills organized") and clear direction ("set up a paperless system that ensures I am never late in paying a bill"). Most likely, the latter statement articulates the outcome with a higher degree of specificity. The second statement makes two things clear: what kind of system you need to implement, and a measure for success.

Do Your Research

Help in selecting technological tools is abundant. You simply have to look in the right place. People can be a great source of information, but you also need to listen carefully to what they say about a product so that you can:

- Understand what they have learned about the product.

- Understand how they have learned it. (Did they read articles, and which ones? Did they talk with people, and whom? Have they used the product, and used others as a point of comparison?)

- Hear exactly what their experiences have been with the product (it broke after a month, it scared my cat, etc.).

- Understand what their goals were in using the product, so you can understand whether their goals were similar or different from yours.

- Weed out statements that begin with "I'm not sure, but I think it will . . ." or "I heard from someone, I can't remember who, that . . ."

One way we use the results of talking research—since it can be as valuable as it is subjective—is through a method we call "triangulation." If we hear the same idea or recommendation from three unconnected people we respect, we go with it.

Here are the sorts of people you can chat with to research purchasing a product:

A techie friend. Do you have a friend who seems to be running a help desk for their friends and family? Ask their advice on a prospective purchase; they'll love it and you'll reap the rewards—a win-win situation. They might also then be very helpful to you once you purchase the product. Ask people you may expect to know the answers. College and high school–age students grew up with technology, so it's practically second nature to them. For basic computer questions, or more difficult technology problems, the younger generations' technology savvy could help you solve your technology troubles.

Other people with the same dilemma. This is the fun part of this research—talking with people! Find someone with the same dilemma you have, and ask this person how they solved it. For example, ask other soccer moms at practice if they've used an electronic calendar and if so, which one? You may also happen upon a stranger using a product you're considering purchasing, and politely ask that person a few questions, such as, "Do you like your cell phone? Do you find it has good reception?"

You can also research a product by looking at the product's Web site for more detailed product specs or by looking up a third-party product review on sites like CNET.com or Gizmodo.com.

Determine Whether Your Gadget Will Fit into Your Life

Once you've satisfied yourself that the gadget or program will actually help you reach your desired end state, the next thing to consider is how easily the tool will fit into *your* life.

What do we mean by "fit into your life"? Designers and programmers create tools that reflect their way of thinking about a problem and its solution. Their way may or may not be your way. Think like Frank Sinatra—your goal is to say "I did it my way." Hopefully, you can find a tool that supports you in that goal. For example, the people who developed the iPod had a way of thinking about cataloging music that led to the basic structure of the tool. They thought it made sense to store digital music files in a giant "library" that can then be organized and viewed on the basis of song, artist, album, or genre. Probably one of the reasons the iPod is such a hit is that this organizational structure fits with the way most people want to access their music. But what if you had two very different collections that you didn't want to comingle—one with music and the other with the spoken word such as Books on Tape and motivational tapes. If you put them all in the same library and hit "shuffle" (the function that plays each digital track or file at random), you'd be just as likely to hear the chapter of a book as you would a song. Now that's fine, if you don't mind hearing random snippets of stories in between songs. But if that isn't your cup of tea, you need to work around the existing structures to get the device to do what you want it to do, or, at the very least, know about the downside before you purchase the product and are eventually disappointed. Workarounds take time and energy and all too often fall just short of the mark in terms of desired functionality. When a gadget doesn't really do what you need or want it to, you're not as likely to use it. There you are back at square one.

Ask yourself: will using this gadget require me to completely change the way I would normally address the problem I'm trying to solve? If so—take a pass. You're better off without it. If you're unsure, give yourself a week before you buy it. During that time, think about what you would have to change to fit it into your routine. The answer to that question will point you in the right direction.

Learn from an Expert

If you find you need help from an expert, the first place to look is in your gadget or computer warranty. Many of them come with (or you have paid extra for) on-site or local help services. If this

Warning: Danger Ahead— Remember to Back It Up

Being Buttoned Up means being prepared. On that crucial note: if you have a new computer, this is an excellent time to get prepared for when your computer crashes (because sooner or later it will). We *strongly* suggest you invest in a backup disk drive or remote, online backup service and save your updated files to it frequently (ideally once a day, but at least once a month). Many programs allow you to set up an automatic time or trigger for the backup, for example 5:00 P.M. every day or every time you turn the power on. This ability to set it and forget it means you'll be able to harness the paperless power of computers without having to endure any undue anxiety about losing precious files or documents on your computer.

is not the case then you can look for a paid expert who may be an independent consultant. You find these in the phone book under a heading such as *Appliance Repair* or *Computers and Computer Equipment—Service and Repair* or through the store where you purchased the product in the first place. One service that gets rave consumer reviews is Geek Squad (www.geeksquad .com). You can even pay extra for immediate service calls.

You may also find an unpaid expert. For example, you might go back to the friend who assisted you in purchasing the product in the first place.

Alternatively, you may just need to get some help in thinking outside the box in how to solve the problem by asking someone who is never afraid to try out every single feature a product has in the search for a solution. The ideal type of person for this job may be in your home. Your husband may be happy to help. Or, you might need to negotiate his aid by taking over one of his chores for him. Kids in the 10–17-year-old age group were born with technology that we had to learn as adults, and often can solve the problems we can't. So don't forget to ask your kids for help!

Getting Help

1. If you decide to call a paid expert, first try and make the problem go away yourself by powering the item down and up again. You can do this by unplugging and replugging, rebooting your computer, or taking a battery out and putting it back in. This solution works in many cases. If you can, save before you power down.

2. If the problem is still there, write down every message you see and what button you pushed to get to your

stuck state. The expert will surely ask you for this and you'll be ready!

3. To avoid frustration, determine your initial plan A and a backup plan B before you begin troubleshooting. Plan A might be: "I have one hour to figure this out, after that, I'm going back to my old phone" or, "I have the whole afternoon, I'll do whatever it takes to get my hard drive up and running again!" A plan B might be, "If I can't fix my hard drive, I'm going to cry for twenty minutes and then go shopping for a new computer *and* a backup drive."

When to Let Go of Old Technology

Americans threw out 315 million computers in 2004, and 100 million cell phones in 2005, according to a *Booklist* review of *Made to Break: Technology and Obsolescence in America*[2] by Giles Slade. Those numbers represent one computer for every single person in the United States, and one cell phone for every three people!

Sometimes we need to get rid of not-so-old products because they were built with poor-quality materials in the first place (planned obsolescence). More often, we trade up because companies stimulate their sales by stimulating our dissatisfaction with the old and desire for the new (psychological obsolescence).

Therefore, it's common that the device you bought yesterday will be trumped by another product or a new version of the same product in six to twelve months. So rather than chase the latest, most exciting version of something, ask yourself: what do I need it to do today? Will data need to be transferred? What will be involved in the upgrade? Once you understand the changes you'd have to make and if the upgrade will significantly improve your use of the product, it's easier to stop obsessing about what you might get in the next-generation release.

If you determine that a device would only be useful as an organizational tool if there was a significant change in the functionality, design, or both, don't buy a stopgap tool for the interim period. Put it out of your mind until such an advance occurs and find a low-tech tool in the meantime. Or alternatively, if you've got entrepreneurial leanings, you could try to create a product that actually addresses your need!

Use Technology to Minimize Overload and Pinch Points

Technology can often be an aid to make sure the critical areas of information in your life continue to flow easily. In this section we will examine each area and suggest several software and electronic solutions you might want to consider for helping you get the job done.

#1: The In-box

This in-box collects all of the communications to, from, and with every member of your family. It is the channel for voice mail, e-mail, snail mail, BlackBerry messages, text messages, instant messages, and Web pages. With so much information coming in, it's easy to get overwhelmed and not get the information you need. The following are some easy ways to put technology to work on your in-boxes so that you can stay in touch with the rest of the world in a way that works for you and not the other way around.

1. **Set up filters:** Virtually every e-mail program has embedded filtering technology. Putting those filters to use is one of the simplest ways to streamline your in-box with minimal effort. The beauty is that if you take a few minutes to set up ones that work for you once, your mail will automatically be "sorted" for you when it comes in—making it one less thing you have to worry about! Use the rules and alerts tools in your e-mail program to move messages from high-priority recipients directly to sub-folders that are easy to monitor. Turn on the junk mail filter! If you have a Palm or BlackBerry, separate your e-mail from phone settings so you don't jump like a Pavlovian dog every time the thing buzzes (try making your phone buzz, but your e-mail silent).

2. **Consolidate:** In this digital age, you can receive faxes and voice mails in your e-mail in-box. Sign up for a voice over Internet protocol (VoIP), or a phone line that will e-mail you all voice messages. We also find it is incredibly useful to have an electronic fax number. This service accepts your fax for you, scans it, and e-mails it to you. That way, wherever you are, you get the fax right when it comes in and it is already in an electronic format that is easy to store on your computer. A good service to try is eFax (www.efax.com).

3. **Delete and file:** Schedule time at the end of every day (three to five minutes) to delete all of those e-mail messages that you don't need to save. Put the messages that you do want to save for future reference in a file folder so you can easily access them later.

4. **Schedule time to turn it off:** It's hard to concentrate when you're constantly bombarded with messages. Try to turn

BlackBerrys and instant messaging programs (IM) off and close e-mail during scheduled times of the day (it's generally easier if it's the first thing in the morning, lunch, and/or end of the day). Schedule it in your calendar as work time. If you can't fathom disconnecting every day, try it for two or three days a week.

5. **Electronic bill payment:** Almost every bank offers this service and once you have set up all of your monthly bill information, paying your bills each month will take just a few minutes. Discuss any security concerns with your bank, but we both have paid our bills electronically for several years now and have not had any issues.

#2: The Schedule

The schedule is the pipeline for everyday obligations, appointments, extracurricular activities, and special events for everybody in the household. Setting up a personal calendar electronically is a straightforward proposition. It's an easy way to keep track of all of your daily or weekly schedules and maintain your contact list.

However, when it comes to keeping track of family schedules, electronic calendars are not yet as good as paper-based products. That's because in order to function well everyone needs to have easy access to the information. This either means a family computer needs to be in a place that is in the center of the family activity (e.g., kitchen or den), always on and always online, or everybody needs to update, or sync, their individual calendars with a master calendar at least once a day. Neither of those options is ideal. We've searched high and low and we have not yet

Just What Is VoIP Anyway?

VoIP, or voice over Internet protocol, is the routing of phone or voice conversations over the Internet. VoIP allows you to make calls over the Internet for low or even no cost. It also allows you to have portability of your number when you are on the road as long as you have broadband access. VoIP also has many of the popular phone features you are used to, like call waiting, voice mail, and call forwarding.

There are, however, a few watch-outs with VoIP. Emergency calls cannot currently be traced to an address via VoIP. There is an emerging standard to fix this but for now, if you dial 911 using VoIP, the operator will not be able to trace your phone location. In addition, if the power goes out and you lose your Internet connection, your phone will also not work.

Two popular services to try are:

Skype: www.skype.com

Vonage: www.vonage.com

found a perfect solution to the electronic family calendar. So, when it comes to staying on top of schedules, you're better off keeping at least one paper or whiteboard calendar that the whole family can use.

#3: The Chores

Chores keep the home functioning and clean. How do you keep track of who does which chores, and when? How are they rewarded? The following products can help you with these challenges.

1. Excel or Microsoft Word: An easy way to manage the chores for everyone in the household might be with a simple spreadsheet or table that you can update, print, and post each week. It should list the person and the tasks and note what needs to be done by when.

2. Use a computer program like My Reward Board (www.myrewardboard.com) to customize and then print out your chore chart. This might be especially effective for young children who enjoy seeing their favorite character, such as SpongeBob, at the top of the list of their chores.

3. To get the chores done by your children (or even your spouse), you might try incentives, rewards, or, as we sometimes call it, bribery. Try Handipoints at www .handipoints.com. Parents set up the chores and related points online and when the tasks are completed, parents can hand out the reward points (purchased from the site), which can be redeemed for online merchandise.

#4: The Stuff

The stuff pertains to the physical possessions of each person in the household. Technology can be a helpful tool to not only electronically store your stuff but also as a way to sell and get rid of excess stuff. The following are a few of our storage and resale favorites.

1. **Sell extra stuff on eBay:** Go to www.ebay.com and set up an account. It is very simple to make money by selling the items you want to get rid of. Not enough time or

energy for that? Go to one of the many eBay stores, drop off your items, and let them sell the item for you on eBay. You pay them a commission and you are done. Or, ask your kids to do it and give them the commission.

2. **Photos:** Store your digital photos on your computer by date or even subject. Try out Picasa (www.picasa.google .com).

3. **Music:** Organize your digital music with what is quickly becoming the standard program: iTunes (www.apple .com/itunes/).

4. **E-cards:** If you don't have time to always send a paper card, try an e-card. One site we like is www.egreetings .com. The site will even send you reminders of your family's upcoming birthdays.

Technology can be a tremendous time-saver and a welcome tool for getting your life organized. Just remember, it can be challenging to change your daily habits and routines. The technology that is right for you will fit into the way you already live your life. Before you commit to any new technology—a gadget or program—research it enough to know that you will be able to use it and that it will do what you want and need it to do.

Button 6: Put Technology to Work for You

When technology works for you, productivity goes up. But when it doesn't, things can quickly grind to a halt.

Don't expect perfection! A technological tool that's new (first generation) might have great features, but might not have the bugs worked out. Don't wait for the latest to get started.

Know the objective. Try and state your goal in using technology to solve your problems in terms of desired results or outcome.

Do your research. Talk to others, including a techie friend or others with the same dilemma. Listen when others talk about what they have learned about the product, how they learned it, what their experiences have been, and what their goals were in the first place.

Choose a tool that won't require a change in the way you normally address the problem. It should fit into your daily routine, not vice versa.

Hire an expert or enlist a friend to help you with setup or troubleshooting.

Technology can help you keep an effective home control center:

The in-box. Set up filters in your in-box technology (junk mail filter in e-mail, folders for storing e-mail), and consolidate by getting a VoIP to e-mail your voice messages. Remember to delete and file each day and schedule time to unplug so you can recharge (your brain, that is) and focus.

The schedule. There's no perfect family calendar—use paper!

The chores. Use a spreadsheet or word processing program to update the chores list and print it each week.

The stuff. Sell extra stuff on eBay, organize photos using Picasa, use iTunes to digitally organize music.

File It Away

Maybe something like this has happened to you. It is 8:15 A.M. and you are running out the door, coffee in hand and already late for work. Suddenly you realize that you have once again forgotten to give your son's immunization records to the school office. Without them, he can't go on the class trip and you know he'll sulk for days if other kids get to go and he can't. You run back in the house, quickly open your Pottery Barn wood filing cabinet and start searching frantically. Is it filed under his name? Under immunizations? Under the doctor's name? Or is it not filed at all? You stumble upon your last five years of electricity bills, that article on travel to Bhutan, and even the roster from last year's Little League team, but no immunization records.

When you're an hour late to work, you call the pediatrician's office and sheepishly explain that you have once again misplaced the records. "Yes," you say, "I know they were faxed to me last week and that your office is filled with sick kids. But if you fax them to me once more I promise I'll never call and ask for than ever again. I think. Probably. Hopefully."

If you've ever "temporarily misplaced" (i.e., lost) a paper, not filed a paper, or filed it and lost it in a morass of file folders, you're not alone. If you would prefer sitting with your mouth open and your legs up in a nice comfortable seat in the dentist's office (without Novocain) to the torture of dealing with papers and a filing cabinet, we hear you.

There has to be a better way to keep track of important information. There is. According to the National Association of Professional Organizers, people waste an hour a day—roughly twelve weeks a year[1]—searching for information they know they have but they cannot get their hands on. Unfortunately, one of the biggest offenders for keeping information accessible is the filing cabinet.

The problem is not filing, it's how we file. Are you someone who:

- Files away so much information that it is difficult to find what you need?

- Files nothing and keeps everything in piles, stacks, and boxes? One study has found that "pilers" encompass nearly half of the workforce.[2]

- Has adopted a filing system that is just too cumbersome and complicated to find important information quickly?

No matter what filing system you are using, this chapter will help you organize your most important information, show you what items you can toss, and give you options on what you can do with the information you want to save. What's more, the process will be relatively painless and so satisfying you may even notice you're starting to enjoy yourself. You may even find your paperwork efficiency nets you BU Time—the time to "be you" that is the fruit of being Buttoned Up.

We have also included something in this chapter for people who want to keep certain information handy but are not sure how to store it. We call it a YUNK box. It's a great new time-saving concept that works. More on that later.

Mountains of Paper

Ellen used to live near the mountains. Mountains of paper, that is—in her home. Almost every year, Ellen and David moved and each time more and more papers and files moved with them. When they first got married, they kept a small two-drawer metal file cabinet in their spare bedroom. By the time they celebrated ten years together, even six files drawers were bursting at the seams. David used to joke that they were at the point where they moved more file boxes than wardrobes for clothing.

Something had to change when they moved to Manhattan. There was no longer endless space for their hundreds of files, filing cabinets, or mountains of paper. They had to take action and conquer the paper mountains.

Fast-forward to the present. David and Ellen have found a system that works for them to manage all of their important information. This chapter explains how the filing system works so you can set up your files using the same efficient system that Ellen and David created when they were faced with limited space but a need for keeping track of all of their information. That's one option for you.

The Foolproof Filing System

There are three easy steps to setting up a simple and effective filing system so that you can find what you need when you need it. Start thinking about what you would like to do with the hours each week you'll save by not having to search for missing information.

Step 1: The Top Ten List

We have found that one of the keys to locating information quickly is to limit the numbers of files you have in your active or daily filing system to ten. Before you panic, we have been doing this for a long time and having ten files is not only doable, it's even liberating. Do not worry; we will help you to deal with what to do with everything else later. For now, you will be setting up your essential filing system.

Start by finding an empty file drawer or buying a filing box. Then get ten hanging folders with labels. Label nine file folders as follows:

- Family information

- Medical (including records and immunizations)

- Insurance (life, medical, auto, homeowner's)

- Legal

- Financial/Money

- Home

- School

- Work

- Taxes

It is up to you how to label the tenth folder. It can be anything except *miscellaneous* or another catchall phrase. Examples of what some people have chosen include *valuables*, *auto*, *real estate*, *travel*, or *emergency planning*. Your insurance folder can include subcategories for each part of your family's insurance; medical, homeowner's, and car insurance policies. Believe it or not, for most people, these ten categories are sufficient to file all of their most important information. This is our 80/20 rule in practice and if you give it a try, you will see that it works.

Step 2: Sort It

Now that you have set up your filing system, you need to sort through all of the documents and files that you have now. We suggest you set aside three or four hours for this process, as you have probably accumulated a lot of loose papers by now. That may seem like more time than you have. If you don't see any way to block off a four-hour window, schedule two two-hour ones. It simply isn't realistic to think you can make enough of a dent without at least two hours. Get four large baskets or boxes and label them *trash*, *top ten*, *active*, and *inactive*.

- *Trash*, of course, will get tossed or recycled.

- *Top ten* refers to anything that fits into the ten file-folder categories you set up in step one.

- *Active* is for other files that you use once a quarter or more. For example, you will want to keep medical information and bank statements at your fingertips for now. These files will be kept separately from your ten files so you can use them frequently.

- *Inactive* are the files that you want or need to keep but do not look at on a regular basis. These papers will not be included in your ten file folders. Store these out of the way so they do not create clutter around the papers you will need.

As you sort through all of the papers and documents in your file folders, ask yourself the following questions to help you determine in which box to place your documents. Depending on your "pack rat" status you can decide whether you would need a larger space/file box.

1. **Is this item current or do I have a more up-to-date version to keep?** Often, we keep multiple versions of similar items that take up space (e.g., saving your insurance policies year after year instead of only keeping your current one).

2. **Can I find this information somewhere else? Can I throw it away?** Do you have online access to this information so you do not have to keep paper copies (e.g., credit card and bank statements, investment transactions, and newspaper clippings)?

3. **Do I need to keep it all?** Oftentimes you can throw away large sections of a document. Take a quick glance through the document. If you have already attended the event, know the information, or have it on your calendar, pitch that section of the document. The more you can throw away, the less information you have to sort through to find things.

4. **How often do I really need to have access to this information?** Be honest with yourself about this. If you don't look at it regularly, put it in the inactive box and get it out of the way.

Once you are done sorting, take each category and give it a home.

1. Take the top ten file information and dispense it into the appropriate file folders. This is now where you should go to look for your most important information. Once a quarter, go through these files and purge them of unnecessary information so that you can still easily find information that you need.

2. Sort the active box into files and store them in your home office or den, separate from the top ten. That way you have access to information you need, but it is not in the way of your most critical documents. Be sure to label the files clearly so you know what's in each and you'll be able to find what you need.

3. Finally, the inactive files can be stored anywhere you have the room—basement, closet, or attic. Wherever you store them, get them out of the way and out of sight, but accessible if you should need them one day.

Step 3: Collect YUNK

The final step to getting your files in order is to create a YUNK box for yourself. A YUNK box isn't yucky or junky in the slightest—it's just the opposite. What is a YUNK box, you ask? YUNK stands for "YoU Never Know" and it is a place for "you never know" items that may need to be held on to "just in case." It can be a cardboard box, a drawer, or a plastic file cabinet. A YUNK box helps eliminate the stress of throwing out something that may be valuable but captures clutter and keeps it out of the way, yet accessible in case it is needed.

Melinda has a YUNK box in her home office. It is a fabric-covered box with a lid that holds all of her extra items like articles to read about helping Kate, her daughter, sleep through

How Long to Keep Important Information

The following chart gives you some general guidelines as to how long you need to keep your important documents. You can always check with your lawyer or accountant for more specific details.

Document	How Long to Keep
Bank statements	6 years
Birth certificates	Forever
Canceled checks	6 years
Contracts	Until updated
Credit card account numbers	Until updated
Divorce papers	Forever
Home purchase and improvement records	As long as you own the property or are rolling over profits from it into new property
Household inventory	Until updated

the night, two holiday cards and letters she wants to keep, extra pictures from her cousin's wedding, and a list of ten-minute ab exercises to try when she has time. Melinda and Stan go through the YUNK box about once a month on a Sunday night when it starts bursting at the seams.

Vivian, on the other hand, keeps her YUNK box in the family room. It is a large plastic box with a locking lid. In it this month are coupons for products she wants to buy at the grocery store, her three-year-old's endless supply of beautiful art

How Long to Keep Important Information

Insurance, life	Forever
Insurance, car, home, etc.	Until updated
Investment records	6 years after tax deadline for year of sale
Investment certificates	Until cashed or sold
Loan agreements	Until updated
Military service records	Forever
Real estate deeds	As long as you own the property
Receipts for large purchases	Until sold or discarded
Service contracts and warranties	Until sold or discarded
Social Security card	Forever
Tax returns	6 years from filing date
Vehicle titles	Until sold or disposed of
Will	Until updated

she makes at preschool, and a few pictures that need to go in frames. Vivian has been keeping her YUNK box for over a decade.

Button 7:
File It Away

Ask yourself if you have one of the major filing problems: filing too much, keeping everything in stacks and boxes and not filing, or a filing system that is too complicated to find important information quickly.

Buttoned Up Filing:

Step 1: Limit the categories in your active/daily filing system. The top-ten filing categories—things to have quickly on hand—include family information, medical, insurance, legal, financial/money, home, school, work

Step 2: Sort your papers into *trash, top ten, active,* and *inactive.* Top-ten files should be easily accessible in your office space. Store active and inactive files away from the top ten.

Step 3: Collect YUNK—a box for papers that "YoU Never Know" whether you'll need or not, but want to hold on to for a while just in case.

Write It Down . . . Cross It Off!

The director of medicine at a community hospital in a medium-sized Texas city was fuming at the thought that she had been stood up. She was waiting to interview a brilliant young doctor who was flying in from New York, who she had hoped would become her new fellow. She looked at her watch; he was thirty minutes late. She started making phone calls, starting with the program director from the city hospital who had recommended him. Did the big-city doctor think he could just blow off interviews? Pretty soon she went from angry to worried. She couldn't reach the resident on his cell phone or his pager. She called others who knew him. They all said he was always responsible, on time, and on the ball. Had he been in an accident?

Then she got the call. The resident was in Buffalo, New York, not Waco, Texas. And he was mortified. He had gone to the wrong interview!

How did that happen? The way we heard this story was the resident had received the phone call about the interview when he was working and in the midst of chaos. There were five people clamoring for his attention. So he "uh-huh'd" and "yeah'd" his way through the appointment discussion with the administrative assistant and willed himself to remember the details. When he got home at 2:00 A.M., he scribbled what he could remember of the conversation in his date book and went to bed.

He didn't have the phone number of the administrative assistant who had phoned him, and he was too sheepish to call around to get the correct information, so he built his travel and interview plans around the incomplete information he had written down. So there he found himself, four months later, in the wrong place at the wrong time and totally humiliated.

Because of all of the calls to reach him, his boss and his colleagues all knew about his screwup. His embarrassment was so deep that he couldn't get himself to reschedule and go to Texas for the interview. He apologized to the director of medicine and told her he had written off the hospital as a choice and eventually he received his third choice for placement. To this day, he is still extremely distressed about the whole situation.

Has something like this happened to you? Have you ever forgotten to write something down or transcribed the information incorrectly, only to end up in the wrong place at the wrong time and/or dropped the ball on something critical? You may never find yourself in a position as drastic as that of the young medical resident. But if you are not in the habit of writing things down and keeping the notes in a place where you can find them when you need them, important details will fall through the cracks.

You can avoid this predicament by writing things down—

virtually or physically. The act of capturing important details, to-do's, and thoughts is a fundamental organizational skill and definitely part of what it means to be Buttoned Up.

The Secret to Alicia and Sarah's Effective List Systems

Note-taking and list-making styles are as personal as the way you dress or cook. Whichever way you choose to write things down, most likely you feel positive about lists: 85 percent of the 339 women we surveyed agree with the statement "I like to make lists and make them frequently; they help me feel like I've got things under control."[1]

It's the same for us. We both have systems that work for us and help us stay in control of the hundreds of business and home details we keep track of each month. But we each have very different systems.

You probably have your own system too. We'd never suggest you drop your system and take up one of ours. But for some reason, we're guessing you are dissatisfied with your own system. Do you lose lists? Do you have too many? Do you write them and not cross things off? Do lists make you feel more anxious, rather than clear and capable? Do you tend to focus on your life day-by-day, and get lost when it comes to the continuity of using lists on a weekly or monthly basis?

The following information may help. We looked closely at both of our very different systems, and found where they overlap. We may do things differently, but we think similarly when it comes to getting things done. Years of trial and error and a common love for efficiency and effectiveness led us to the same place—systems that work for us.

Here are our four principles for keeping effective written notes and lists:

1. Write it down immediately in a place just for daily lists and notes.

2. Write it all down—both personal and work, big picture and detail.

3. Rewrite routinely to consolidate, prioritize, and focus.

4. Review your list every morning.

Write It Down Immediately in a Place Just for Daily Lists and Notes

An idea comes to you as you're biting into your tuna salad sandwich at lunch. It might be a huge lightning bolt like, "I think I'd like to see if we could swing a family trip to Hawaii next year" or a small grumble of thunder like, "I think I'm due for a teeth-cleaning appointment." What do you do?

You might simply make a mental note or start scribbling on a paper napkin. We're sure there are great inventions that started that way, but that's not the method we're recommending here. Here's our recommendation: write it down in something that you've earmarked specifically for your ideas and lists.

This might sound basic, but it's really a huge, important step. Why? Because those haphazard notes and lists on a sticky note posted near your computer screen or desk so you "don't forget" are really just a source of distraction and stress. They're distractions because they keep you from focusing on what you have to do. For example, you're finishing up your week's report in the office, and every once in a while you glance at the Post-it on your monitor and think "Buy milk" and "Pick up the dry cleaning," which then can morph into "What are we going to have for dinner?" or "What other errands are on the way to the dry cleaner?" Pretty soon, fingers that were tapping on the keyboard as you focused on writing the week's report stop typing and now you're staring at a hangnail and thinking about chicken marsala. Your attention to your writing is shot. Whenever you're distracted, you're less productive and can end the day saying to yourself, "What did I do today?" In a recent study, a group of Microsoft workers took, on average, fifteen minutes to return to serious mental tasks, like writing reports or computer code, after interruptions. So, reminder Post-it notes are just a bright source of anxiety instead of a helpful reminder. It is especially stressful if you have fluorescent pieces of paper all over your desk and computer. You will feel more stressed if you constantly think about what you have to do, and in turn not get your work done.

Besides distractibility, the other problem with random notes and lists is that they're focused on the short-term. They rob you of your ability to look over everything on your list and choose priorities—what's really important to you—and make a plan on how to accomplish your priorities each day, week, and month. Planning also gives you the opportunity to consider which tasks on your to-do list you'd like to delegate. For example, in Carol's daily lists, she includes her delegating to-do's next to a person's name, like "Matthew: Contact Our Financial Planner." (For more on delegating, read Button 3: You Don't Need to Do Everything Yourself.)

What We Use

Sarah uses a notebook. "After a lot of experimenting with different formats and programs, I have settled on using a simple, lined, eight-by-five–inch journal that is easily portable. That way, I have it whenever and wherever I need it. Sometimes, if I'm feeling the need to recapture a bit of my youth, I mix it up and buy a regular three-hole-punch spiral-bound notebook like I used for note-taking when I was in school.

"I tried taking notes virtually for a while, using the task section of my e-mail program. But I was always on the go, and that just wasn't handy for me. I even tried one of those portable hand-held gadgets that you could sync to your e-mail program, but somehow writing in hieroglyphics wasn't really my forte. I never got the hang of it, which meant I never used it, which meant I was always missing important details. Now as long as I have my little notebook with me, I am golden. I use it for notes, lists, phone numbers—anything and everything I need to remember."

Alicia favors legal pads. "For me, legal pads are the answer. I've used them for as long as I can remember to keep track of my to-do's. I have several on hand at any one time to help me keep track of the different areas of my life: family, work, and me. I love the feeling of accomplishment of ripping off a page when I have completed a long laundry list of things to do."

Some people choose to combine all their lists into one master list and keep it with them at all times in case they have a moment at work to complete a family task, like call the electrician or order the cake for a birthday party. For some people, it may work better to leave their work list at work, home list at home, and "me" list in their purse. It is entirely up to you to determine the most effective way for you to keep your lists. Do what works for you and you're more likely to stick to it.

Alternative Ways to Write

You might need to scribble on a napkin if it's impossible or inconvenient for you to write something down immediately in your regular daily list and note-taking place. Remember, though, to transfer the information to your regular daily list location as soon as you can—within twenty-four hours is a good rule of thumb. There are many ways you can "write things down." A few of our favorites are:

- Keep a pen and paper handy at all times—at home by the phones, at work in your desk, in the car and in your purse. Have many pens and paper at the ready to jot information, ideas, and to-do's down.

- Purchase a small voice recorder so you can "write" things down by just talking into the machine. Some people love this and find it the easiest way to temporarily capture important information until they can get the information onto their list.

- Write to yourself. Send yourself a text message or an e-mail to remember important to-do's. This may work well at work where you are on your computer.

Write It All—Both Personal and Work, Big Picture and Detail

Once you have a place for your notes and lists, whether it's a journal, a legal pad, a computer file, or a PDA (personal digital assistant), you need to figure out a way to keep track of both the big picture and the details for *everything*: your family, your work, and you personally. The reason it's important to manage more than just the usual task-specific details and keep an eye on the bigger picture is simple. If you follow through on the things that you write down, then choosing *what* to write down means you're in charge of shaping your life. Both Alicia and Sarah keep their work and home to-do lists separate. That means when they're at work, and want to review their priorities for the day, they can simply look at to-do's for work and not be distracted by what needs to be done at home, and vice versa.

Not writing something down can actually be limiting. We like to say, "what gets written, gets done."

Jacquie learned that lesson the hard way. Jacquie is very driven professionally and tends to be a bit of a workaholic. She always meticulously follows her job-related to-do lists to move the ball forward professionally. But she never really got in the habit of keeping a list for herself. Jacquie tends to value spontaneity in the rest of her life, almost as an antidote for her determination and focus at work. So she'd get to the weekends and just wing it. It turns out, Jacquie found, that that's not such a great way to go.

As life got more complicated and busy, Jacquie realized it became harder and harder to get together with friends on the spur of the moment. And then there was vacation. Every year, right around the middle of July, her husband would ask her about the long-awaited family vacation. But Jacquie would be so overwhelmed with tasks on her to-do list for that week that she'd throw her hands up and throw out the possibility of a long weekend somewhere in October. But since she didn't keep track of her personal to-do's, that would inevitably fall through the cracks. Then in October, Jacquie would be too busy to take a vacation, and would throw out the following April as a possibility, and so on, and so on. That destructive cycle went on for years.

Only when she made a conscious effort to start writing down personal to-do's, like vacation planning, in addition to her work tasks, was she actually able to plan and take a real vacation. The only way Jacquie is actually able to be spontaneous is to plan for it! Now she simply takes the time to dream a bit about what fun things she wants to do with her husband, her child, and her friends. She keeps a running list of the ideas she comes up with in her journal and then makes them happen by incorporating them into her to-do lists. With this simple planning on her lists, Jacquie was able to plan a trip with her sister to Quebec, and to buy concert tickets for her husband's favorite band.

You can keep a running list or have categories within your lists. Think of them as buckets to catch what is slipping through the cracks. Work-list categories could be inventory, administration, or publications. Sarah says, "Occasionally I will add one area or take one away, but for the most part they represent the strategic pillars of my business and/or home life. As such, I'm thoughtful about making sure my framework still makes sense once or twice a year. Are the 'buckets' correct? What's missing? What's not essential anymore? Because each of the buckets that I use to organize my to-do lists represent strategic pillars, it's much easier to think ahead, about the present *and* the future simultaneously."

Rewrite Lists Routinely to Consolidate, Prioritize, and Focus

The third principle for keeping lists and notes efficiently is to rewrite your lists routinely at a regular time—daily and/or weekly.

Alicia keeps daily lists (one for work, one for home). Every morning, before she does anything else, she rewrites each list onto a new sheet in her pad, and gleefully tosses out the old lists with an arcing swish into the trash can. Each new list eliminates cross-outs from the day before and adds new to-do's generated by the previous day's notes, messages, and voice mails. "I can't start my day and go to the bank unless I've written *bank* on the day's list."

Each Friday she rewrites her master lists (again, one for

work, one for home). In her master lists, she keeps track of to-do's that may not need to be done tomorrow or even next week, like buying chairs for her new office or looking into summer camp for Lucy.

Unlike Alicia, Sarah doesn't keep a daily list. Each Sunday afternoon she steals away to her desk and creates a new weekly list on the computer. She edits her old typed list and adds items from her handwritten lists and notes in her notebooks. She prints out her weekly list, folds the sheet in half, and carries it around in her notebook as her guide for the week. Each time she makes a new weekly plan she tosses last week's printout. Letting go always creates space for the new.

Rewriting lists is very helpful in staying on track and reducing stress. Rewriting the lists helps to:

Consolidate—Eliminate the messy cross-outs and distracting Post-its and add new items from many different sources onto one list.

Prioritize—Three or four priorities for the week can be at the top of your list. Rewriting is also an opportunity to think about priorities.

Focus—With a clean, current list, you can get started quickly and focus on the task at hand, instead of trying to figure out what the next task will be.

Clearly notice what's not getting done—If something has been carried over from week to week on the to-do's without ever getting done—it's time to reevaluate. If it is critical, set a deadline and commit out loud to people that you will have X done by Y date. Once you do that, it's virtually impossible not to get it done. If it isn't critical, take it off your list completely. Having nonessentials on the list not only takes the space from the other important items, it acts as a nagging reminder of something left undone—even if it's not very necessary. Eliminate it from the list to make room for essentials.

Review Your List Every Morning

Looking over your lists each morning before you start your day—daily or weekly—will help you remember the 80/20 rule and focus on what is most important to accomplish that day. This review need not take more than three minutes but it is worth the time to get the day off to a productive start.

Starting off the day tackling your priorities will get you off to a good start and keep you from getting bogged down with the stuff that doesn't matter. Many of us have so much to do that it would be impossible to get everything done. Our strategy is to try to knock off something you've been dreading first thing—most tasks will be easier if you take care of the tough one first.

Making Your List System Work for You

Think about what has and hasn't worked for you when it comes to keeping notes and lists. Determining ineffective systems is the first step toward making a new start and picking a system that *will* work for you.

1. Choose your note-taking and list-making location—what do you like to write in? What will you be able to carry with you the most often?

   - A spiral three-hole-punch school notebook
   - A bound blank writing journal

- A legal pad

- A computer file

- A PDA

- Other _____

2. Choose whether you would like to:

- Keep a daily and a weekly list

- Keep only a weekly list

- Keep only a daily list

3. Choose the time for your weekly list creation:

- Every morning

- Every night

- Friday afternoon

- Sunday afternoon

- Monday morning

- Other _____

Now, visualize using your new system—for example, holding your notebook, writing in it, using your to-do list, and rewriting it. Walk through the process, thinking about what has worked for you in the past with your lists, and what hasn't. If you can visualize your new system and it works, try it out slowly, observing what is working and changing things as you need to.

Once you get your note-taking and list-making system working smoothly, don't keep it to yourself! Share your system with your friends and relatives, like you'd share your favorite recipe for pineapple upside-down cake or banana bread!

Button 8:
Write It Down . . . Cross It Off

Success depends on using four principles for keeping effective
written notes and lists:

1. Write it down immediately in a place just for daily lists
   and notes.

2. Write it all down—both personal and work, big picture
   and detail.

3. Rewrite routinely to consolidate, prioritize, and focus.

4. Review your list every morning.

The choices you make during planning allow you to clarify
your priorities and consider which tasks on the to-do list you'd
like to delegate.

Choose your note-taking and list-making location—What
do you like to write in? What will you be able to carry with
you the most often?

Choose the frequency with which you will write a to-do list:
daily, weekly, or some combination of both.

Choose a regular time and place to write your weekly list
creation.

Happily Buttoned Up

Getting There and Staying There

Once you are happily Buttoned Up, then what? To answer that question, we want to go back to the early days of our business. The phrase "happily Buttoned Up" came out at one of our business brainstorm meetings over coffee and scones with Sarah and Alicia and Alicia's sisters, Susan and Nancy. Although no one remembers who actually said the words, we all agree that time stood still the second they were uttered.

Those words helped us make a huge mental shift. They allowed Sarah to reframe her old concept of being organized from an either "you are or you aren't" static goal to a flexible and positive state of mind. Says Sarah, "I used be a yo-yo organizer. I'd go in fits and starts, vacillating between being a big mess and being the picture of pulled together 'fabulosity.' Once liberated from the tyranny of one, single image of what it meant to be organized, I no longer felt like a failure. My new way of looking at things felt comforting and supportive: one messy kitchen day and one missed appointment didn't mean I wasn't organized."

But there is even more to it than that. Like getting fit, we see getting happily Buttoned Up as both a goal and a process. Even the smallest action—like putting up a family bulletin board and calendar—can start you toward your goal of getting happily Buttoned Up. It's not like the goal of driving to New York, where once you're there, you're there. When it comes to getting happily Buttoned Up, once you get there, you have to do something to stay there. How can you maintain the condition?

Once you are liberated from the monolithic and nearly unattainable "chore" of *getting organized,* it's relatively easy to incorporate a few simple things into your daily routine that will ensure you stay happily Buttoned Up over time.

What will help *you* stay happily Buttoned Up and focused on maintaining your new habits? Here are some ideas.

Maintain a Healthy Perspective

Just as there is no magic pill that will help you achieve and then maintain a perfect body, there is no organizational system that is a magic stairway to being perfectly organized all the time unless you substitute "imperfect" for "perfect." Your ultimate (and ongoing) success requires embracing the notion of Imperfect Organization. Start with *you.* Once you've articulated what success means for you, you can accept that there are going to be days where you'll be more "organized" than others. It won't be the end of the world or mean you've plunged into chaos. You can start over the next day and use any mistake as a learning opportunity.

You're your own best cheerleader in your goal to stay Imperfectly Organized. To support yourself and stay positive, try some of the following tips.

Notice Changes

When you're getting fit, statistical proof of change abounds—it's on the scale, in the number of repetitions of an exercise that you can complete, on the clock when you keep track of your minutes of cardiovascular activity, or at the doctor's office when you learn about your improved cholesterol levels.

Mileposts denoting change may be a little more subtle when you're getting happily Buttoned Up, but they're quantifiable nonetheless. Pay attention. Did you:

- Put something away in its "home"?

- Consciously *not* do something and accept that it *won't* get done?

- Review your priorities and your list this morning?

- Take time to relax with your kids without thinking about what you're *not* doing?

- Accomplish more than usual without panicking?

- Throw out something that you usually would save?

Any or all of these are Buttoned Up milestones. Savor them. Take a minute to feel great about it!

"The journey of a thousand miles begins with one step" is a beautiful Chinese proverb that applies here. Noticing your positive steps toward change (however small) may sound like a silly thing to do, but can be very powerful. Here's an example: Have you ever driven on "autopilot" and been surprised to find yourself somewhere familiar that you didn't intend to go? Part of the problem was surely that your mind was elsewhere—thinking about work, a spat with your spouse, or what you were going to cook that night.

Contrast that with paying attention to your directions and the road signs carefully with your destination firmly in mind from the moment you start out. The latter, both when driving and when getting happily Buttoned Up, is the method we'd recommend to get to where you want to go.

Reward Progress

Okay, you notice you're improving. The house is neater. You're feeling less stressed, and have fewer headaches. There is less yelling, more smiling for you, your spouse, and the kids. You're feeling happily Buttoned Up.

Don't let this improvement go by unacknowledged. Reward yourself and others for making changes. A psychologist would call this positive reinforcement; so would a dog trainer! We just think of it as a pat on the back—for yourself, and your family.

Think about rewards you and your family would like, both small and large. Here are some ideas:

- Treating yourself and a friend to a coffee date

- Taking a hike in a beautiful neighborhood area

- Giving yourself an extra hour to just goof off with the kids

- Getting a pedicure

- Cooking or eating some of your favorite foods

- Purchasing something new

- Taking a weekend away

- Going out to the movies

Don't let your change go unnoticed . . . be your own biggest cheerleader. Let your family know what you are celebrating if you cook a special meal. The positive reinforcement you will receive will encourage you to stay happily Buttoned Up. Don't forget a lot of encouragement for the other members of the household too!

Build In Your Own Organizational Checks and Balances

When it comes to fitness, you may have your own way to check your status . . . your jeans are too tight, you're not in your preferred weight range, or you are not able to run or walk as far or as fast as you used to. When it comes to being organized, consider what your own organizational checks are, and then how you handle them. For example:

- If you repeatedly can't find items that you're looking for in a room, it's time to straighten up the room! Remember to identify the one or two tasks that will make the biggest difference in organizing that room, and tackle those first.

- If you miss an appointment, you might start paying particular attention to each new appointment you make and look back at the missed one to figure out why it happened to prevent it from happening again.

- If your home feels chaotic, have a "family meeting" to make sure the Control Center and chore list are up-to-date.

Sarah has her own special organizational check. "If I carry a task over because it didn't get completed the week before, it's a data point that indicates I either need to reevaluate my top

twenty percent of tasks or ask someone else for help. Or both."
Use your lists as a benchmark to check your organizational status. If you are carrying lots of tasks over, or aren't completing
the higher priority tasks, you should refocus on what was successful for you in getting Buttoned Up.

Write It, Read It, Say It, Write It Again

Staying focused is a powerful tool. You may find that tasks you
thought would take you one hour can really be accomplished in
twenty minutes if you effectively block everything else, and we
mean everything, out other than the job at hand. The best way to
"clear the decks" in your own mind is to make sure that your lists
are complete and up-to-date. Having the lists at hand will allow
you to relax and trust that everything is getting taken care of. It
also gives you a place to put those ideas or to-do's that may in-
trude when you are busy with another task. Put it down on your
list, get it out of your mind until you have the time to deal with it.

In summary, we recommend that you:

- **Write** everything down that you need to do on your lists.

- **Read** them every morning, review your priorities,
  schedule to-do's as needed.

- **Talk** with others about how you're handling your lists.

- **Rewrite** your lists daily or weekly.

Maintain a Support Group

The final, essential component of staying happily Buttoned Up
is to remind yourself that you do not have to do it all alone. You

can and should ask others for support and help on your journey. Not only will others be great cheerleaders when you need a boost, they can make it possible for you to do much, much more—although you're actually doing less.

Rely on Your Loved Ones as They Rely on You

Team up. Whether it means asking your spouse, your children, friends or coworkers, or some or all of the above: enlist help! Try to identify sources for both physical and emotional support. Physical support ranges from your children and spouse doing chores around the house to having a running or workout partner. Emotional support is getting that extra hug at the end of a long day or talking to a close girlfriend about your frustrations with getting organized. The physical support will help you actually complete tasks every day, while the emotional support will give you the strength and willpower to get Buttoned Up. You have a perfect right to ask. Here are some surprising statistics on how much housework women, men, boys, and girls typically accomplish.

Women are actually doing half as much housework as they did in 1968, but according to Frank Stafford of the University of Michigan Institute for Social Research, working women today do an average of twenty-five hours a week of housework—that's about 1,000 hours a year.

To be fair, since 1968 men have doubled the amount of housework they do, but there's still a huge disparity between men and women. Men are now doing seven hours of housework a week—still less than a third of the time working women spend.

The statistics from the University of Michigan on boys and girls ages 10–17 show that their time spent working in the house is also glaringly lopsided. The study shows that girls spend more time doing housework than they do playing, while boys spend about 30 percent less time doing household chores than girls and more than twice as much time playing. Also, according to study director Frank Stafford, girls are less likely than boys to get paid for doing housework.

How can your loved ones help? When you're overwhelmed, ask them to pitch in. (For more on how to do this, see Button 3: You Don't Need to Do Everything Yourself.) And talk with your friends and family about your frustrations and success in organizing different aspects of your life, home, and family. If you're talking with your girlfriends, we're sure you'll find an empathic and willing ear!

"Who You Gonna Call?"

Remember in the *Ghostbusters* theme song the words "who you gonna call"? They proposed you call Ghostbusters, but we're guessing your everyday needs are a bit more . . . shall we say . . . realistic? The real question is: Have you ever felt the need to delegate to others when you didn't have the time or the talent or the supplies to get a job done, but you delayed because you didn't know the right person for the job?

One way to avoid procrastinating or delaying when it comes to delegating is to put together a services and house emergency list ahead of time. This extensive list should include all contact information for companies or people you have hired in the past who fixed or improved your home. Remember to write down phone numbers for your electrician, plumber, cable company, lawn maintenance company, and cleaning service. When you have a list in place, you have the person to call when you're in a crunch because you realized your guest-tub drain is blocked and your in-laws are coming for a visit tomorrow.

Having time on your side when evaluating services can also give you the ability to find services at a price that works for you. You may also want to inquire with your insurance provider about getting appliance insurance, which would mean one call and one price could handle a multitude of household problems.

Get recommendations! When you are talking with friends, relatives, neighbors, and colleagues, ask them for recommendations of professionals or workpeople in any of the areas that you may need. To show your gratitude for their help and as one incentive for them to take the time to make thoughtful referrals, consider sharing the completed list with them.

You might want to search out recommendations for:

Job Type	Name and Phone Number
Accountant (especially needed at tax time)	_____
Appliance repair	_____
Auto mechanic	_____
Babysitters	_____
Bookkeeper	_____
Cab company	_____
Carpet cleaners	_____
Caterer (simple or fancy)	_____
Computer technician	_____
Contractor	_____
Dentist	_____

Doctor/Pediatrician _____

Handyman _____

Housecleaners _____

Housepainter _____

Lawyer _____

Plumber _____

Secondhand shop/Company
to haul away "junk" _____

Tailor/Seamstress _____

Typist _____

Window washers _____

Yard workers (lawn,
landscaping, snow removal) _____

Friends and acquaintances can be a big help in maintaining your progress. They want to help too. All you need to do is ask them.

Button 9: Happily Buttoned Up

Maintain a healthy perspective and accept there are going to be days where you'll be more organized than others. Remember, you can start over the next day and use any mistake as a learning opportunity.

Success at staying organized over the long term is much easier if you stick to the three Buttoned Up rules.

1. Maintain a healthy perspective and accept there are going to be days where you'll be more organized than others. Remember you can start over the next day and use any mistake as a learning opportunity.

2. Stay focused on what is important and pay attention to the things you decided mattered, such as putting something away in its "home" or reviewing your priorities and lists each morning.

3. Nurture a support group for yourself—whether it be your spouse, children, coworkers, or friends—to talk about your lists and get help if you're overwhelmed.

Establish organizational checks and balances to stay on track, for example a missed appointment may pay attention to why it happened and your plan to prevent it from happening again

Reinforce teamwork. Reward yourself and your family for changes with something that is new and fun, such as a favorite food or a night at the movies

Consider calling a service. Ask friends and neighbors at get togethers for their favorite accountants, appliance repair, auto mechanics, etc., and then share your list with others.

Button 10

Take the Buttons to Work or School

At the Buttoned Up office overlooking a busy street in Ann Arbor, informality and comfort rule. Visitors are welcomed with chocolate, coffee, and bottles of spring-water. But there's one cardinal rule that visitors are told immediately: no liquids on Alicia's desk. Alicia says, "I was in such a rush to get started in my new office that I didn't take the time to set up a backup drive. Then, the first week in the office, I knocked over a water bottle on my desk and watched as my computer drowned right in front of my eyes. It never booted up again. A big part of being Buttoned Up is being prepared for problems, and you better believe that when I bought a new computer, I bought a backup drive with it. That was the day I got Buttoned Up with my computer."

Take a moment to sit back and congratulate yourself on your own efforts to become Buttoned Up. Have you been able to make changes in your life, big or small? Do you feel a bit more relaxed? Have you once and for all banished the notion of color-coordinated closets and perfectly done scrapbooks? We certainly hope so! We also hope that you have not only learned a new way to think about getting organized but have also taken some of our tools and integrated them into your life and schedule.

In this chapter, we will summarize the Buttoned Up principles and show how you might take them into your work life and to your kids as well. Here's one last review of our brief but powerful list of Buttoned Up principles:

1. Let go of perfection.

2. Focus on the most important 20 percent of organizing tasks and forget the rest.

3. Share the load! Learn to delegate effectively.

Living by these principles will give powerful, positive momentum to your life. The more that you and those around you can be Buttoned Up, the more free time you will have to enjoy yourself.

Incorporating the Buttons into Your Work Life

Most people are as passionate about work as they are about their families and homes. Fortunately, the buttons can help them maintain that intensity in both places, while acknowledging and accommodating the differences between the two environments.

Unless you're self-employed, you likely have a boss at work whose job it is to evaluate your performance. In some ways, the stakes for not being organized are higher at work. While you may have a perfectionist boss, you can still let go of perfect in the way you approach a given task. The 80/20 rule definitely applies and the good news is that you may find the work environment is also geared toward delegation—helping to get the job done by using a team approach.

But whether you use the buttons at home or work, one thing is certain—not being organized is stressful, and can take its toll on your personal happiness. That's where Buttoned Up principles can help—by facilitating your efficient work practices so you can leave the office and "have a life" with less stress in your head and work in your briefcase.

Doing a Good Job Doesn't Mean Being Perfect

For some, applying this concept to work at first seems counter-intuitive. Don't I want to be perfect at work? How can I be good at my job if I am not perfect? Ditching perfection doesn't mean doing an inadequate job. It means focusing on the things that will drive the business or get the job done. Alicia has many examples of how letting go of perfection actually allowed her to be more effective and productive on the job. Here are just a few:

My PowerPoint sales presentations—Says Alicia, "I have all of the most important pieces of data, but I no longer waste two or three hours to get the graphics as perfect as possible. The presentations look good and more importantly the substance is there."

Our sales brochures for a trade show—"They were going to cost double to be collated at the printer's. Instead of doing that and wasting money, we let buyers pick up the relevant individual sheets of information they wanted when they came to our booth at a show. It worked," says Alicia.

Forecasting our sales—"The one thing you can say with certainty is that any sales forecast is going to be wrong. It is just that, a forecast. So trying to be perfect at this is a waste of time. I just do my best to get a reasonable estimate and spend the rest of my time trying to actually make the sales happen," says Alicia.

Focus on the Most Important 20 Percent

Alicia's inspiration for focusing on priorities came from her work experience. Then she actually "exported" the concept to her home life. Specifically, we're talking about the Pareto Principle. Pareto noticed that 80 percent of the consequences stem from 20 percent of the causes—meaning that if you can identify the 20 percent of your tasks that are most influential and focus on them, success will follow. This may mean focusing on particular clients, product lines, projects, locations, publications, classes, problems, or individuals. Only you know what will work for you to move your work goals forward.

In addition, Sarah and Alicia use these methods to focus:

Weekly meeting—Each Monday they talk about their goals for the week and also what they are *not* going to do that week.

Weekly list—Each Sunday or Monday they individually write their own lists of work to-do's for the week, as we describe in Button 8: Write It Down . . . Cross It Off!

Daily list—Every day Alicia rewrites her daily to-do list; Sarah rewrites her list each week.

Morning review—Every morning they each review their work list.

Share and Delegate

As Buttoned Up grew, the number of employees went from one to nine. This jump in head count was essential but required that Alicia and Sarah learn to delegate and avoid micromanaging the process. For example, they both turned over the office management reins to Anne Marie Furie, the Buttoned Up chief juggler, who has significant experience in this arena. By delegating to someone who wanted to manage the office more than they did, Alicia and Sarah essentially gained time and improved Buttoned Up's performance.

On the job, you may delegate or share the workload with an employee, colleague, consultant, student intern, or temporary worker. Either there will be someone assigned to the project or you'll need to search out some help.

When getting ready to delegate, we recommend these four steps:

1. Try to find the right person for the job.

2. Set out a clear objective and timeline.

3. Make expectations and rewards clear and offer support.

4. Give them the job and the time and space to perform the job their way.

Integrating the Buttoned Up principles into your work life will make you more efficient and effective. Take a lesson from Sarah and Alicia: prioritizing, ditching perfection, and delegating will get your career moving and leave time to enjoy life outside the office. For more information on delegating, read Button 3: You Don't Need to Do Everything Yourself.

Kids Can Use the Buttons Too

Another way to utilize the Buttoned Up philosophy is to teach these principles to your kids so that they learn early on how to efficiently organize and manage all of the information, clutter, and appointments that are sure to come their way. Think of it as a gift to them. Probably the best age to pass these buttons on is around middle school or when your child is starting to manage information flow for him- or herself.

Alicia and Sarah are both moms, but their kids are too young right now to benefit from the Buttoned Up way to get organized. Alicia, however, has a niece, Marissa, who is now a senior in high school who has embraced getting her life Buttoned Up.

Helping Them Ditch Perfection

Alicia didn't have any trouble helping Marissa understand that ditching perfection allows you to spend more time doing the things you enjoy. This is perhaps the default mode for many teens. What was new to Marissa was the concept of not feeling bad about ditching perfection but working hard to get the best grades she could and then letting other things go that are not value adding (i.e., the perfect Photoshop art for the cover of a book report).

To help your kids assess the value of perfection, chat with them about whether a desire for perfection will help them succeed in school, and how.

Here are some examples of the ways kids strive to be perfect but not to their advantage.

Wearing perfect outfits—Wearing this year's fashion, high-end labels, and a new outfit each day. Ask, "What is your goal in looking perfect, and will it get you where you want to go?"

Perfect friendships—Does the goal of having a perfect girlfriend, boyfriend, or best friend derail your child's studies?

Perfect sports records—Sports are healthy and fun, but unless your child wants to play a sport in college and wants a college scholarship to pay for school, an impeccable sports record may not actually help your child achieve his or her goals.

Avoiding Distractions and Learning to Focus

Alicia and Marissa worked on this rule together to figure out how best to apply it to school. While it is simple on the surface—focus on the most important things in school and let the rest go—letting anything go at school can be a challenge. Marissa wondered, "Does that mean I shouldn't do sports or drama?" Alicia answered, "No. The most important twenty percent for school is all about learning the most important things first." Your child will need to choose how to focus his or her school energies. Marissa's choice was to spend her time first on her most challenging subjects, math and chemistry, and less time on the subjects that came easy to her, literature and French. She also used the 80/20 rule when applying to colleges to focus the most time and attention on the schools that were her top choices.

Kids Like to Both Get Help and Give Help

"Sharing" with others in school can be a dilemma—if you think about plagiarism, passing notes, or peeking over another's shoulder for answers during a test.

However, there are positive opportunities for students to delegate so that they can spend time on the things with the most value. Marissa used this rule when it came to babysitting. She delegated or gave away babysitting jobs when she needed to study for finals. She also asked her parents for help with her laundry when her school load was heavy. Nobody minded pitching in to help her and she was able to get better grades because she could focus on school.

Another way to delegate or share the load is with studying. Kids can study with friends, parents, tutors, and often teachers offer study sessions during lunch or after school. The skill of actually asking for help when it is needed can be an important one for a student to learn.

The discussion here about children brings us back to the beginning of this book, and our original idea about why women could benefit from being Buttoned Up. Teaching your children to apply the Buttoned Up principles to organization will help them lead less stressful lives and grow into productive and organized adults. Happy and organized kids are one of many payoffs of getting your life Buttoned Up.

Health Benefit to Being Buttoned Up

It turns out that free time isn't just fun and satisfying, it's also stress reducing on a biological level. A landmark study from UCLA in 2000 found that stress releases a hormone in women called "oxytocin" that gives us urgings to "tend and befriend," i.e., enjoy the company of our children, family, and friends. And once we satisfy those urgings, our reward is the release of more oxytocin, which further counters stress by producing a calming effect.[1]

Ahhhhhh. A positive, healthy cycle where getting Buttoned

Up reduces our stress and yields more time to reduce our stress even more. Where does all this lead? Back to where we started . . . sitting down for a good chat with old friends. But this time there's a difference—this time your conversation isn't about your life being out of control. Now, you can talk about where you're going for the next family vacation. Relish that sweet time. You earned it.

A Note from Alicia and Sarah

Before you close the back cover on our Buttoned Up world, sustain your momentum and convert your thoughts to action now by trying at least one exercise. We wish you success in your continued journey to Imperfect Organization. Remember to share your journey with the ones you love and keep in touch. We'd love to hear your Buttoned Up success stories! Write to us at yourlife@getbuttonedup.com.

Buttoned 10:
Take the Buttons to Work or School

At work, the three Buttoned Up rules can help you make progress in the right direction.

1. Doing a good job doesn't meant being perfect, it means focusing on the important 20 percent.

2. To focus on the important things, use your weekly meeting, weekly list, daily list, and morning review.

3. Share and delegate to others by finding the right person for the job, setting a clear objective and timeline, making expectations and rewards clear and offering

support, and giving individuals jobs they can succeed at in a way that works for them.

For your children, the three Buttoned Up rules can be effective tools for instilling the right organizational habits.

1. Chat with your kids about whether a desire for perfection will help them succeed in school, and how. Some ways perfection works against kids is the striving for the perfect outfit or perfect friendships.

2. Help kids focus on their most important 20 percent in school. For example, this might mean studying more in their most challenging subject.

3. Talk to kids about how they can delegate their daily load by studying with friends or helping them out with their chores when it's needed.

Getting Buttoned Up is not an easy task! While we provided you with the most essential tips and tricks throughout the chapters of this book, you still may have some organizational questions unanswered. If you've conquered the trouble rooms, the Control Center, the files, and the tech search, read on for tips on how to Button Up the finer pinch points of life.

Home

Question: My closet is always a mess! Any quick solutions to organize my closet disaster?

Buttoned Up Solution: Here are three easy steps that will help you transform your closets from dumps to diamonds in no time:

#1: Sort It Out. The first step in the process, sorting, actually makes the biggest difference in taming the closet chaos. Take everything out and put it into one of three piles: *keep, toss,* and *recycle/give away.* As you plow through the clutter, stay focused on that 80/20 rule—your keep pile should be 20 percent of the items and the other two piles should comprise the remaining 80 percent. As a rule of thumb, if the item hasn't been used in the past year, it should go in the toss or recycle/give away pile.

#2: Create a Flexible Framework. Three things matter to people when it comes to storage and closets: can I see what I'm looking for, can I reach what I need easily, and is there more than one "right way" for me to put something away. Think about who will use the closet and how they will use the items in it. If some items need to be easily accessible to children, be sure to put them in a low spot. If linens are likely to be put away by different people, give each family member a shelf and label it with a brief description of their bed linens.

#3: Get Help. As you put items back in the closet, especially communal ones, ask other family members to help you get the job done. The time investment they make is likely to pay dividends because they'll be more likely to maintain something that they helped clean up in the first place.

Question: My work area is always cluttered with papers and mounds of mail. Any suggestions for a long-term solution to keep my desk organized?

Buttoned Up Solution: Tame your desk disaster with these simple tips:

#1: Contain Clutter Piles. Clutter piles spread like weeds when you have no containment strategy. Buy a simple basket or in-box and force yourself to put any and all loose papers, mail, and notes into the basket. When it is full, rather than letting it overflow and pile on your desk, deal with the items in the basket immediately. Create three piles: *toss, file,* and *record*; and deal with each accordingly. It should take at most ten minutes to get to the bottom of it all.

#2: Give Everything a Home. Items like pens, paper clips, binder clips, highlighter pens, telephone notepads, and tape dispensers all take up precious room. In addition to restricting your paper piles to a basket, try keeping these desk accessories contained in either a drawer or desk caddy. That way, you have the benefit of a clear desk *and* you'll waste less time hunting around for them when you really need them.

#3: Keep a Notebook. Most paper clutter can be reduced by keeping an office notebook. A simple notebook can be the perfect place for keeping daily or weekly to-do lists, jotting down phone numbers, taking notes, and just generally staying on top of details. Using one will also likely reduce the amount of time you waste looking for lost numbers and Post-it notes with bits of information. Just remember to force yourself to look back at the notebook for the first few weeks until it becomes a habit.

Question: The bathroom countertops and drawers are so messy my family can never find what we need. Any ideas on how to arrange personal items?

Buttoned Up Solution: Here are three things to consider in getting your bathroom Buttoned Up:

#1: Create a Top-Ten Drawer for Each Person in the Family. Assign each person in the family a separate place or drawer for his or her own stuff in the bathroom.

Label each drawer with the person's name using masking tape and a Sharpie marker. Then explain to everyone that they can keep *up to a maximum* of ten items in this space. Items eleven and up have to go someplace else. This is the key to keeping the bathroom neat once you spend the time to organize it. If this sounds tough to do, test it on yourself. Even after you cover the basics: toothbrush, toothpaste and floss, face wash, moisturizer, hairbrush and mousse, and deodorant, you should still have one or two other items you can toss in.

#2: Clear Up Bathroom Storage. The key to knowing what you have in your bathroom is being able to see it. Go to your local super-center or organizing store and purchase a supply of clear containers for bathroom storage. Caddies or baskets with handles are particularly helpful to give each person in the family to keep their shower and tub items in, like shampoo, soap, and conditioner.

#3: Countertops Are Shared Space. Empty countertops are one of the keys to having a tidy bathroom. Keep a maximum of three items on your bathroom counter. If something is going to remain out, it should be something that more than one family member uses on a regular basis.

Consider items like hand soap, Q-tips or cotton balls, or toothpaste. The more you can store away, the better your bathroom will look.

Question: I am looking for ways to expand my storage and make my laundry room cleaner. How can I make the space more functional?

Buttoned Up Solution: Here are a few ideas about how to get the most out of your laundry room:

#1: Make the Prework Easy. Save time and effort by having your family members presort their clothes for you. Put three separate labeled baskets in the laundry room: one for whites, one for colors, and one for dry cleaning. Have each family member drop their laundry in the correct basket. Then all you have to do is just pick up the basket and toss in the wash.

#2: Get Help Putting Clothes Away. You can also easily get help from the family once the laundry is done by having each person in the family put away their own clothes. Purchase a rolling basket stand and have one basket for everyone in the family. Putting folded clothes in each person's basket will save you endless miles of running up and down the stairs to put everything in its place.

#3: Don't Forget the Extras. Finally, don't forget to purchase these small items to get your laundry room all Buttoned Up:

1. **Trash can:** For lint, dry cleaning bags, etc.

2. **Finders-keepers box:** Put those coins and receipts you find in various pockets and pants here to be reclaimed later. Any coins that are not reclaimed after two weeks should go into a treat fund for you (manicures, anyone?).

3. **Bulletin board:** Tack up labels or special instructions for garments that you do not want to forget.

Question: My garage is the trouble spot of my house; it is always messy. How can I utilize the garage to create more storage space?

Buttoned Up Solution: Follow these three easy tips to help you get that gorgeous garage in no time:

#1: Pitch It. Realistically, every garage has old roller skates that are too small, flat tennis balls, and newspapers tucked away collecting dust. Figuring out what items need to be tossed or donated to charity should be your first order of business. Make three piles: *keep, toss,* and *give away.* Follow the rule of thumb that if you haven't used it in eighteen months, it should be tossed or given away. Before you know it, you'll have room for the things you actually want to keep.

#2: Up in the Air. In order to optimize space and give your garage an organized look, install a few hooks and shelves. They are an effective way to organize a wide variety of items—and they have the added bonus of keeping things off the floor. Hang a row of hooks along the side of the garage to neatly store bikes, rakes, shovels, sleds, and all other items that easily get in the way. If you place these hooks close to the back of the garage, it makes them easier to use and you're probably less likely to scrape the car.

#3: The Kids' Corner. Designate an area of your garage as the kids' corner to store all of your children's bikes, sports equipment, pool toys, and arts and crafts. This will make it easy for them to get what they need without calling for your help to find their favorite blue soccer ball or other lost item.

Question: When I am hosting overnight guests, I always feel stressed because of the balance of both entertaining and keeping our family schedule on track. How do I stay organized when I am hosting guests?

Buttoned Up Solution: Here are three ways to keep Buttoned Up while hosting overnight guests:

#1: These Are a Few of Their Favorite Things. A great way to let your guests know you are thinking about and excited for their impending visit is to find out a few of their favorites before they arrive. Whether it's their favorite soap or favorite breakfast food, having a few of your guests' favorite things on hand for their stay is a sure way to provide a warm and heartfelt welcome.

#2: To-Do List. Even the simplest and most routine of tasks may escape your attention while you are busy hosting overnight house guests. To keep on top of your to-do's, make a list of your normal daily activities and keep it posted in a highly visible area, such as the refrigerator or family bulletin board. Commit and carve out a block of time in your calendar to take care of these tasks all at once. By doing so, you will be left with more time for the important stuff, like hitting up all those tourist traps with your out-of-town guests.

#3: Balancing Act. While you will probably need to make slight changes in your daily schedule to accommodate your guests, there is no need to put your entire life on hold while they are in town. Chances are your guests wouldn't want you to in the first place. Instead, try and stay focused on the high importance activities. And don't forget to let your guests know of these prior commitments. The thoughtful heads-up will give them a chance to plan out this free time or even take care of the personal commitments they have had to place on hold.

Moving

Question: I am planning a move four months from now; what are some things I should be doing now to reduce my stress in the coming months?

Buttoned Up Solution: Consider these three tips for things you can do months in advance to prepare for your move.

#1: Keep a Calendar. A move doesn't just sneak up on you. The little things that make up a move, however, usually do. When you decide you're moving, the first thing to do is to buy a calendar, mark your move date, and work your way back to the present day. Establish dates by which certain things need to be done, and who exactly should be doing them. By parceling out all the to-do's to different people in an organized (and visible!) fashion, not only do things get done more efficiently, but everyone shares the load, and reduces your stress.

#2: Change Your Address. Starting two months out, save all your mail in one place—credit card and bank statements, utility bills, magazines, etc.—so you have everything at your fingertips when it comes time to make and track your change of address. Use convenient online change of address services such as Moving.com. Or use a fax sheet that you can copy to send out your change of address information to all your contacts.

#3: Get Your Important Information. Visit doctors and other professionals before the move and seek a referral near your new home. Also, request all medical, dental, school, and veterinary records to take with you.

Question: I have never moved before and have no idea how to pack up my house. Any tips for packing for a move?

Buttoned Up Solution: Packing does not have to be a struggle. Follow these tips to pack (and unpack) with ease.

#1: Create a YUNK Box. YUNK stands for "YoU Never Know." Set aside and label one moving box for just that purpose.

You might throw in a remote control that you still have but are not sure what it goes to. Put in those plastic doohickeys in the kitchen that probably make something work. You will surely find a home for some of these things when you unpack at the new place.

#2: Consider What You Need to Open First. Put aside one box for items that you will want to get to first and label it *open me first*. We like to include things like toilet paper, garbage bags, a box opener, paper towels, pens, and screwdrivers. Make sure to put this in the moving truck last so it is easy to get to right away. Once the rest of the boxes are off the truck and the movers are gone, you still have to unpack! One way to simplify that process is by thinking ahead and keeping track of what went in each packed box. You can either mark each box with where it came from/needs to go (kitchen/bedroom/bathroom) or number each box and keep track of its contents on a separate sheet of paper. You'll now have the right boxes in the right area, making it an easier, quicker task to settle into your new home.

#3: Pack a Gift Box! Whether you're single or have a family, take a few minutes to pack a small gift box to open on your first day in the new house. Include some of your favorite items—ones with sentimental value and things that make you smile. Write a quick note to yourself (or have each family member write a note to the entire family) with your wishes for your life in your new home and your top five favorite memories of your old home.

Technology

Question: My digital pictures are a mess! Any tips on how to straighten up my digital memories?

Buttoned Up Solution: Here are some tips on how to get your digital pictures under control:

#1: Pick a Program. Whether it's iPhoto or Kodak Picture Viewer, test a few different photo viewing programs until you find one that you really like. Then stick with it. It's much easier to keep track of all of your photos if they are in one place. You're also much more likely to keep them up-to-date and organized if you find the program to be intuitive and easy to use.

#2: Share the Fun. Sending photos via e-mail attachments can be a major time waster, and larger photo files are often stopped by e-mail filters anyway. So store them online instead. Most photo sites such as Flickr, Kodak Gallery, and Sony let you store and create online albums for free. When you're ready to share them with friends and family, simply e-mail the link and they will have easy access without having to sit through a never-ending download.

#3: No Need to DIY. Let the pros handle your digital printing for you. Online services provided by Kodak, Sony, and even CVS let you upload your digital photos and print them for less money than it would initially cost for an old-fashioned roll of film, not to mention the cost of developing that roll of film. The best part: you don't even need to travel to pick them up. Often within a few business days, your printed photos are sent right to your front door, completely hassle-free.

Question: The desktop on my computer is a dump; I can never find what I need and it is slowing my computer down! Can you help with my digital disaster?

Buttoned Up Solution: These tips will help get your computer in shape and keep it that way:

#1: Learn to Share.
There are bound to be files that people other than you will need access to. Instead of sending never-ending attachments or burning stacks of CDs, create a shared folder on everyone's desktop or set up a remote folder on a site like Xdrive that others have permission to access. After you set up the shared folder, simply drag any file in and everyone has instant access.

#2: Out of Sight but Not Out of Mind.
Consider purchasing an external hard drive, flash drive, or backup device. The extra storage space will let you hold on to any outdated files that you don't need immediate access to but are too important to toss. While you're at it, use the external drive as a safety net and back up the contents of your computer. That way you're prepared for any digital disaster!

#3: Routine Checkups.
Just like a garden, your computer is more likely to stay neat and healthy if you spend a little time on the "weeding out" process now and again. So to ensure your files and folders stay clutter-free, commit to routine "bite-sized" checkups. Try taking five minutes on your lunch break or after the kids are fast asleep to delete old e-mails and files.

Question: I wish I could get more out of my cell phone, but I don't know where to start! Any tips for making the most of the organizational capabilities of my phone?

Buttoned Up Solution: Organizing with your cell phone can be a breeze. Following are three cell phone features you must try!

#1: Cell Phone Calendar. Your cell phone calendar is a great tool to remind you of upcoming important meetings or events. Look for it under the tools area on your phone under "calendar" or "planner." It's simple to use. Once you select an appointment date, the phone will prompt you to enter the event details, such as title, start, duration, and when you want the alarm to remind you of the appointment. This feature is perfect for those appointments you have to make way in advance and are likely to forget.

#2: Ring Tones. When you enter in phone book information for new contacts, take five extra seconds to assign them to a caller grouping, such as "family," "friend," or "boss." Once you have distinct groups, you can give them each a ring tone, so you have an idea of who is calling right away. If you're in the middle of something and it's not a ring tone you have selected as urgent, you know you can call whoever it is back later.

#3: Text Messaging. Text messaging is a very efficient way to get an important message to another person when you're not in a position to talk. Look for it in the message area on your phone, then simply create a new message and start typing. Most phones also have a predictive text feature that finishes what word you are typing, so it's fast and easy. If you are likely to send the same message frequently (such as *I'm on my way*), store it so you can use it again later.

Question: I am constantly misplacing, scratching, or forgetting about some of my favorite CDs. Any help to get my music collection organized?

Buttoned Up Solution: Use these tips to organize your collection and get the most of your music:

#1: Go Digital! The era of cassette tapes is over—all music has gone digital. In fact, in Alicia's new home, she can plug her iPod right into the wall to play music throughout the rooms! Make space in your home and car by uploading all of your music on your computer. In addition to providing extra room around the home, going digital organizes all of your music in one spot.

Transfer your cassettes to CDs and then upload them to your computer so you can listen to them anywhere at any time; www.cassettes2cds.com will transfer cassettes and records to CDs and VHS to DVDs for you!

#2: From Aerosmith to Zeppelin. If you want to hold on to those CDs after you upload them onto the computer, organize them so that you can quickly find your favorite artist. An easy way is to organize them alphabetically by artist, but don't forget you can also organize them by music genre or decade as well. Alicia organizes her CDs from A to Z on her bookshelf, while Sarah's music is all on her computer and can be organized alphabetically, by genre, by decade, by date added, or however she wants.

#3: The Playlist. Make playlists instead of CD mixes. This is great for the gym, your kids, and dinner parties. If you are having a hard time pitching a favorite mix that a friend made you, upload it onto your computer and store it as a playlist! If you are in the mood for variety, it is also fun to put your iPod on "shuffle" to randomly select the order of songs or albums.

Finances

Question: I feel overwhelmed when I even think about paying the monthly bills. How do I overcome this feeling and set up a stable system for paying the bills?

Buttoned Up Solution: Once you have picked a day and time for bill paying, follow these simple steps for organizing the process:

#1: Go Electronic. Computers can practically do everything for us these days, including bill paying. You can automatically pay bills every month by setting up electronic bill paying with your bank. All you have to do is enter in the information of who to pay and when, and with a quick confirmation your bank will transfer funds to the payee's account and deduct money from your account every month. This is so simple that in 2005, 24 percent of bills were paid electronically. So jump on the bandwagon and you will never have a late bill again!

#2: Get a System. For those bills that you would rather review by hand, it's important to have an efficient system for accomplishing the task. First, gather all bill paying accessories in one spot. This includes your checkbook, calculator, envelopes, stamps, and mailing labels. Then make sure you have a place for all of your unpaid bills. It's a lot easier when you don't have to search for everything first!

#3: The Aftermath. After you pay bills, label them immediately with the check number and date because you *will* forget what you paid! While you're at it, we encourage you to organize your paid invoices and receipts into tax category folders. Highlight tax-related items on your bills, such as home office purchases or state tax returns, so you're ahead of the game next April. But avoid unnecessary clutter, save only the tax-related paid bills.

Question: I am always so disorganized when it comes to paying taxes. Any helpful hints to make the tax process easier?

Buttoned Up Solution: Try these suggestions to establish a system that's simple enough to set up and use all year long to ensure you are prepared for April 15:

#1: Give Everything a Home. Take fifteen file folders and label them for each of the critical tax categories:

Bank statements	Credit card
Medical/Insurance statements	Work expenses
Other deductions	Other expenses
Dependents	Retirement
Investments	Other income
House bills (mortgage)	Last year's tax return
Property tax	Work compensation
Charitable donations	

Look at your last year's return and talk to your tax preparer about what items specific to you might go in each folder. The final folder should be called *YUNK*. YUNK stands for "YoU Never Know" and is for everything that you think might be useful but are not sure about. File it here now and deal with it later. You are also always better off filing away too many things now and throwing away whatever you do not need later. Re-creating the wheel at the eleventh hour is what takes so much time, adds gray hairs, and raises blood pressure.

#2: Annotate Tax-Related Items with a Star. Credit card and bank statements along with check registers can be a good place each month to record taxable items. Before you file things away, get out a pen and put a star next to items that have tax implications. Things to consider would be charitable contributions, interest income earned, tax payments made, home office purchases, or state tax returns. By highlighting them now, it will be a cinch to capture them next year. If you don't have a tax-related item on your statements—throw them out! You don't need to keep them—keeping unnecessary papers around will just add to the confusion next year and take up precious space.

#3: Visit the IRS Online. Even the Internal Revenue Service knows how complicated the tax process can get. By visiting the IRS Web site at irs.gov, you can get clarification on all of your tax questions, learn what tax laws have changed, and, most importantly, see what does and doesn't qualify as a deduction.

Other

Question: With such a hectic family schedule, I never find time to relax. How can I schedule a couple minutes of peace?

Buttoned Up Solution: Here are a few tricks to help you find (and keep) some BU Time, or time to be you:

#1: Bundle Up. While no amount of wishful thinking will help you escape your weekly errands and chores, there's still a way to make all of your must-do's work in your favor. Try to bundle all of your errands and appointments in as few clusters as possible. Not only will you save tons of time that would otherwise be wasted shuttling to and from your destinations, you'll give your car a much-needed break from all those city miles, which as we all know can really add up!

#2: Seize the Opportunity. Sure, we could all benefit from a little more time in the day (if not to get more done, then for a full night's rest), but there are tricks to help you make the most of the time you already have. Try to line up some spare moments for yourself during family downtime, such as when the kids are busy with after-school clubs or during nap hour. And if conflicting schedules keep you from enjoying a little "me time" (all those practices and play dates never seem to line up in a way that gives you a meaningful break!) hiring a mother's helper a few afternoons a week is sure to do the trick as well.

#3: Keep Everyone in the Know. Once you've managed to secure a little time for yourself, don't forget to let your loved ones in on your personal plans as well. Discussing the details in advance and blocking the time on your family calendar will prevent you from having to ditch your plans at the last minute due to an unforeseen conflict. Then once you're squared away with your family, kick back and relax—it's definitely well deserved!

Question: How do I teach my children to develop organizational habits?

Buttoned Up Solution: Here are three life lessons that are never too early to instill:

#1: The Twelve-Month Rule. Closets are bursting with clothes, 80 percent of which are never worn. Beds overflow with stuffed animals, 90 percent of which are outdated and dusty. Teach your children the one-year rule: if you have not used it in twelve months, chances are you never will. So muster up the courage to get rid of it. Throw it out, donate to charity, sell it on eBay—whatever works for you—just get rid of it. It takes up space and you don't need it.

#2: Technology Is a Pack Rat's Best Friend. Do your kids have piles of magazines, photos, CDs, school projects, etc.? Figure out what your kids love to horde and find a technology solution that saves space and clutter. For example, almost all magazines can now be found online. Why save them? CDs can be put on the computer. Digital photos can be stored electronically and you can even get a scanner to store regular pictures.

#3: Quid Pro Quo. It sounds so obvious, but you'd be surprised at how often this little thing is overlooked. Your kids cannot put things away if they don't have a place to go. Work with them to choose some fun, inexpensive shelves, cubbyholes, bookcases, or storage boxes for their things. Work with them to figure out how to label the boxes, let them pick silly names—anything to make it fun, and decorate the labels you make for each shelf. The more involved they are in the process of defining the structure, the more invested they will be in the process of staying organized.

Question: I am always forgetting friends' and relatives' birthdays and anniversaries. How do I keep track of these special dates without adding clutter to our family calendar?

Buttoned Up Solution: Collecting the information is one thing, but remembering to observe them is another! Here are two easy ways to remember to celebrate the birthdays and anniversaries of the people you love:

#1: Create a Master Birthday Calendar. Whether your main calendar is in a PalmPilot, an e-mail program like Outlook, or on paper, it should be easy to keep track of birthdays. Grab your list, and spend fifteen minutes a day (if that) and put all the birthdays in your calendar for one month. In two weeks, you'll have a master calendar completed. If you're likely to send a card or buy a gift for the person, jot down a note like what gift you got them last year or what size they take in clothing—right in the calendar entry. If you don't happen to keep a master calendar (is that even possible?), buy a birthday book or make a binder of your own. Make sure there's a page for each day of the year—and simply transcribe your list, along with any notes, into the binder.

#2: Remind Me . . . Remind Me and Then Remind Me Again! It's easy to set up reminders in this digital age. If you're using an electronic calendar, set alarms a few days ahead, so you can get a card out in time. Or make an "appointment" to call the person at 9:00 A.M. on their big day. If you don't have time to set your own alarms, sign up for a Web-based greeting service like Egreetings (www.egreetings.com). Enter your important dates and a reminder e-mail is sent to you a week ahead of the date to remind you it is coming up. Also, once the dates are entered you don't have to enter the information again, a reminder will be sent to you automatically each year.

Question: How do you prepare your family for an unexpected emergency situation?

Buttoned Up Solution: Here are three suggestions and tips to follow to help you prepare your family and home for anything unexpected:

#1: Remember the Big Four. Water, food, cash, and a first-aid kit are the foundation of any emergency kit. Make sure you have enough of each of these things to last each person in the house at least five days. Imagine how much suffering could have been avoided in the recent hurricanes if people had prepared a family emergency kit stocked with these necessities.

#2: Engage the Entire Family. Getting prepared should be a family event, not a burden for one person to carry. It's in everybody's best interest to know what's been done and to be invested in the process. Make sure each family member has a job to do and encourage them to get it done within a week. One person can buy flashlights, a whistle, and lots of batteries, another can find a radio (battery operated) in the house and make sure it still works, and someone else can clear out space in the pantry, garage, or basement to store all of the emergency supplies.

#3: Get Extras. Think about any items that are critical to you and that may not be easy to get for a few days in an emergency and have extras on hand. Some important things to consider are prescription medicines taken regularly, glasses and contact lenses, plus saline solution and a contact case, and baby items such as formula and diapers.

Also visit www.getbuttonedup.com/links.htm or www.ready.gov for additional resources.

Resources

Alicia Rockmore and Sarah Welch

E-mail: yourlife@getbuttonedup.com

Web site: www.getbuttonedup.com

MySpace page: www.myspace.com/getbuttonedup

Tips and inspiration: www.getbuttonedup.com/news.php

Blog: www.getbuttonedup.com/blog

Products: See shop.getbuttonedup.com or visit www.getbuttonedup.com for a list of retailers.

Products

BlackBerry
www.blackberry.com

Excel
www.microsoft.com/products
1-800-MICROSOFT (1-800-642-7676)

iPhone
www.apple.com
1-800-MY-APPLE (1-800-692-7753)

iPod
www.apple.com
1-800-MY-APPLE (1-800-692-7753)

Life.doc

www.getbuttonedup.com

1-734-477-5020

Microsoft Word

www.microsoft.com/products

1-800-MICROSOFT (1-800-642-7676)

Mom Agenda

www.momagenda.com

1-877-333-2433

Palm

www.palm.com

1-408-617-7000

Post-its

www.3m.com/us/office/postit

Quicken

www.quicken.com

1-800-811-8766

TiVo

www.tivo.com

1-877-289-8486

Verizon

www.verizon.com

1-800-621-9900

Books and Magazines

Cookie magazine

www.cookiemag.com

1-877-402-6654

How to Organize Just About Everything

Peter Walsh (New York: Free Press, 2006)

www.peterwalshdesign.com

It's All Too Much

Peter Walsh (New York: Free Press, 2007)

www.peterwalshdesign.com

O magazine

www.oprah.com/omagazine

1-800-846-4020

Organize magazine

www.organizemagazine.com

1-888-912-1010

Organizing for the Creative Person

Dorothy Lehmkuhl and Dolores Cotter Lamping, C.S.W.

(New York: Three Rivers Press, 1993)

Quick & Simple magazine

www.quickandsimple.com

1-888-957-3637

Real Simple magazine

www.realsimple.com

1-800-881-1172

Smart Organizing: Simple Strategies for Bringing Order to Your Home

Sandra Felton (Grand Rapids: Fleming H. Revell, 2005)

The One-Minute Organizer, Plain & Simple

Donna Smallin (North Adams, MA: Storey Publishing, 2004)

Online

Amazon.com

www.amazon.com

BigDates.com

www.bigdates.com

1-925-866-4110

California Closets

www.californiaclosets.com

1-800-274-6754

CNET.com

www.cnet.com

Cozi

www.cozi.com

1-206-957-8447

Department of Homeland Security

www.ready.gov

1-202-282-8000

eBay

www.ebay.com

eFax

www.efax.com

1-800-958-2983

Egreetings

www.egreetings.com

Flickr.com

www.flickr.com

FreeConference

www.freeconference.com

Gizmodo

www.gizmodo.com

Google Alerts

www.google.com/alerts

Google Calendar

www.google.com/calendar

Google Docs and Spreadsheets

www.google.com/intl/en/options/

Handipoints

www.handipoints.com

Instant Messaging from AIM

www.aim.com

iTunes

www.apple.com/itunes/

1-800-MY-APPLE (1-800-692-7753)

Kodak Gallery

www.kodakgallery.com

1-800-235-6325 (1-800-23-KODAK)

Lifehacker

www.lifehacker.com

Mamasource

www.mommasource.com

MapQuest

www.mapquest.com

Mommy Track'd

www.mommytrackd.com

Moving.com

www.moving.com

My Reward Board

www.myrewardboard.com

Picasa

www.picasa.google.com

Reclaim Media

www.cassettes2cds.com

1-866-669-6496

Smead

www.smead.com

1-888-737-6323

Snap Fish

www.snapfish.com

1-800-634-4500

Sony.com

www.sony.com

Windows Messenger

www.get.live.com/

Stores/Catalogs

Apple

www.apple.com

1-800-MY-APPLE (1-800-692-7753)

Barnes & Noble

www.barnesandnoble.com

1-800-THE-BOOK (1-800-843-2665)

Bed Bath & Beyond

www.bedbathandbeyond.com

1-800-GO-BEYOND (1-800-462-3966)

Brookstone

www.brookstone.com

1-800-846-3000

Buttoned Up, Inc.

www.getbuttonedup.com

1-734-477-5020

Day-Timer

www.daytimer.com

1-800-225-5005

Flight 001

www.flight001.com

1-877-354-4481

HSN

www.hsn.com

1-800-284-3900

Resources

IKEA

www.ikea.com

1-800-434-IKEA (1-800-434-4532)

Lowe's

www.lowes.com

1-800-445-6937

Office Depot

www.officedepot.com

1-800-GO-DEPOT (1-800-463-3768)

OnlineOrganizing.com

www.onlineorganizing.com

Organize.com

www.organize.com

1-800-600-9817

QVC

www.qvc.com

1-888-345-5788

See Jane Work

www.seejanework.com

1-877-400-5263

Target

www.target.com

1-800-591-3869

The Container Store

www.thecontainerstore.com

1-888-CONTAIN (1-800-266-8246)

Uncommon Goods

www.uncommongoods.com

1-888-365-0056

Wishingfish.com

www.wishingfish.com

1-877-785-3914

Resources

Other

1-800-Got-Junk?

www.1800gotjunk.com

1-800-GOT-JUNK (1-800-468-5865)

FedEx Kinko's

www.fedex.com

Geek Squad

www.geeksquad.com

1-800-GEEK-SQUAD (1-800-433-5778)

National Association of Professional Organizers

www.napo.net

1-856-380-6828

Skype

www.skype.com

United States Post Office

www.usps.com

Vonage

www.vonage.com

1-VONAGE-HELP (1-866-243-4357)

***Wall Street Journal*—the Juggle Blog**

blogs.wsj.com/juggle

WhiteFence

www.whitefence.com

1-866-241-0665

Notes

Button 2

1. J. T. Bond, E. Galinsky, and J. E. Swanberg, *The 1997 National Study of the Changing Workforce*. New York: Families and Work Institute (1998).

2. Joshua S. Rubinstein, U.S. Federal Aviation Administration, Atlantic City, NJ; David E. Meyer and Jeffrey E. Evans, University of Michigan, Ann Arbor, MI: "Executive Control of Cognitive Processes in Task Switching," *Journal of Experimental Psychology—Human Perception and Performance*, vol. 27. No. 4.

3. In December 2006, Buttoned Up, Inc., conducted an online survey of 480 women. The representative sample of female respondents answered more than twenty organizationally oriented question-statements (to be rated on a scale of weight of importance), such as "I keep the majority of tasks and projects I have to do in my head" and "I'm confident in my ability to discern what's important to get done and what isn't." Hereafter this is referred to as Buttoned Up Custom Research.

Button 3

1. Sheila Hutman and Jaelline Jaffe, Ph.D., Robert Segal, M.A., Gina Kemp, M.A., and Lisa F. Dumke, M.A., *Burnout: Signs, Symptoms and Prevention*. Helpguide Mental Health Issues, 2005. http://www.helpguide.org.

Button 4

1. Buttoned Up Custom Research. Customer Survey. 2005. Joint research study on document management best practice conducted by Gartner Group,

Coopers & Lybrand, Ernst & Young, cited by NAPO, est. publication date 2005. http://www.napo.net/press_room/media_stats.pdf on page 20.

2. Gartner Group, Coopers & Lybrand, Ernst & Young, *National Association of Professional Organizers Research*. 2007.

Button 5

1. Kyle Mundry, "American and Japanese Personal Consumption and Savings Habits (Part 1)." Entry for *Moffatt Prize in Economics* (2004).

2. Research by Ann McKinney for National Association of Professional Organizers.

Button 6

1. Peter Lyman and Hal R. Varian, "How Much Information 2003?" School of Information Management and Systems: University of California Berkeley, 2003. http://www2.sims.berkeley.edu/research/projects/how-much-info-2003/.

2. http://www.amazon.com/Made-Break-Technology-Obsolescence-America/dp/0674022033

Button 7

1. National Association of Professional Organizers database mentioning a publication in *Newsweek*, June 7, 2004.

2. Ann McKinney and Sharon Mann, PileSmart Study. National Association of Professional Organizers.

Button 8

1. Buttoned Up Custom Research. (See Button 2, Note 3.)

Button 10

1. S. E. Taylor, L. C. Klein, B. P. Lewis, T. L. Gruenewald, R.A.R. Gurung, and J. A. Updegraff, "Female Responses to Stress: Tend and Befriend, Not Fight or Flight," *Psychological Review*, 107(3):411–29.

Index